EXPRESS, MAIL & MERCHANDISE SERVICE

Jeff Wilson

KALMBACH BOOKS

WAUKESHA, WI

Kalmbach Books
21027 Crossroads Circle
Waukesha, Wisconsin 53186
www.Kalmbach.com/Books

Published in 2016
21 20 19 18 17   2 3 4 5 6

Manufactured in China

ISBN: 978-1-62700-378-0
EISBN: 978-1-62700-379-7

Editor: Randy Rehberg
Book Design: Tom Ford

Unless noted, photographs were taken by the author.

Library of Congress Control Number: 2016938936

Contents

"MOFFAT ROAD"

WHITE & BOWER
WHOLESALE
HAY 2120

1

CHAPTER ONE

History of merchandise, express, and mail service

An Adams Express Co. horse-drawn wagon is backed up to the Denver & Salt Lake (Moffat Road) depot in Denver around 1900. Several crates and barrels of LCL and express can be seen on the platform. *Trains magazine collection*

Today, the local railroad station is just a memory, and it's the step vans of UPS and FedEx that roll up to your house or storefront business to deliver packages and express parcels. If you have a business that needs to ship a pallet or two of goods, you'll call the freight divisions of those companies or a trucking line such as Con-Way, Old Dominion, Estes, or R+L Carriers, all of which provide what's known as LTL (less-than-load or less-than-truckload) service. Retail stores now receive their wares by those services, by the truckload from wholesalers and distributors, or directly from manufacturers.

The Nashville, Chattanooga & St. Louis freight station in Chattanooga was one of hundreds of terminals around the country where LCL freight was transferred and reloaded among boxcars. *NC&StL*

Mail now travels by truck or plane, and although some does indeed still travel by rail, it's in sealed trailers and containers that ride atop railcars, and clerks no longer sort mail inside specialized cars as trains roll along.

From the horse-and-wagon days of the mid-1800s into the 1950s, railroads were the main provider of all these services, **1**. Railroads gave the best rates to companies that could fill an entire car with a load, while charging a higher rate for smaller items and shipments. Railroads then packed these smaller shipments into cars, consolidating them for movement to common destinations. The result was that the overall tonnage was comparatively low, but the potential profit margin for less-than-carload (LCL) traffic was high because of the multiple shipments traveling at higher rates.

Each railroad operated its own LCL service, which was tied to other railroads by an extensive network of freight houses and transfer stations, along with tens of thousands of local railroad depots across the country, **2**. Thousands of boxcars operated in LCL service, all following strict schedules and routing. They operated in freight trains but—although at slower speeds—with coordination matching passenger trains. Tens of thousands of workers were needed to keep this traffic flowing smoothly.

For expedited service, individuals and businesses alike would call for a pickup from Railway Express Agency (REA), which had a monopoly on the country's express service. One of the company's ubiquitous green trucks would arrive shortly to get the shipment on its way, **3**. The service garnered a premium rate (often double) compared to common LCL service, but it was faster, traveling via baggage cars on passenger trains of any of the country's railroads. From the 1920s onward, air express was also available through REA.

So whether it was a Christmas present from Aunt Edna in Sacramento to her nephew in Atlanta, a toaster from Sears in Chicago to a family in Pocatello, Idaho, or a replacement piston for a tractor engine traveling from the Case Co. in Racine, Wis., to an implement dealer in Kearney, Neb., railroads were more than likely involved in the shipment.

Knowing what types of items were shipped; how parcels, express items, and mail were handled; what kinds of cars and equipment were used; and how railroads routed cars and scheduled their trains help modelers better duplicate these operations in miniature. Let's start with a brief look at the history of railroad express, LCL, and mail services.

Beginnings

The U.S. Post Office was well established by the time railroads began expanding throughout the country in

Railway Express Agency's green delivery trucks were familiar sights across the country through the early 1970s. Here, a driver poses with his Diamond T truck around 1930. *Jeff Wilson collection*

the mid-1800s. Carrying mail by rail was economical and drastically cut down on transit times compared to horse-drawn stages. Letters that once took weeks or months to travel a few hundred miles now could be delivered in several days. The early 1860s saw the introduction of the Railway Post Office (RPO) car, in which clerks sorted, delivered, and picked up mail in transit. Combined with mail storage cars, this service would continue through the 1960s, **4**.

Sending packages was another matter. For the most part, sending a package meant contracting with a private courier—an expensive proposition—or an express company. Express companies found their niche by collecting parcels at one location, grouping them together, shipping them to a common destination, and then dispersing them for delivery.

The first of these express companies, fittingly, was the First Express Co., which was started in 1839 by William Hernden. A former railroad conductor and agent, Hernden is generally credited as the father of the express business in the United States. Hernden began his business as a one-man operation, carrying small

parcels himself in a carpetbag between New York and Providence, R.I., via steamship. The service proved popular, and within a few years, his expanded company was carrying express parcels on railroad cars from New York to Boston and other cities.

Hundreds of express companies soon emerged across the country, using a combination of railroad cars, steamships, and their own horses and wagons. The most famous early service was the Pony Express, which used a relay of riders on horseback to carry mail (not parcels) from St. Joseph, Mo., to Sacramento, Calif., making the journey in 10 to 12 days. Although the service only lasted 19 months after its April 1860 debut, the Pony Express certainly helped establish a level of adventure and intrigue for the express industry. (It was made obsolete by new technology—the first transcontinental telegraph line.)

Early major express companies included Adams Express, which started in 1840 and quickly covered the East Coast and Southeast, eventually adding lines to St. Louis and expanding west; Wells, Fargo & Co., which was founded in 1852 (but had roots in older companies) and

was soon providing express service to California; and American Express, based in New York and started in 1849.

The country's population continued to grow and expand westward, and did so quickly after the Civil War as railroads extended their routes throughout the country. The first transcontinental railroad was completed in 1869, and a web of rail lines soon spread out across the Midwest, Pacific Northwest, Southwest, and Plains states.

Small express companies found that they couldn't compete against larger companies, and many either merged to stay competitive or went out of business. Railroads—which were also merging to form larger companies—aligned themselves with various express companies, which allowed the express companies to claim specific routes and mileage.

In 1890, there were still more than 30 express companies reporting mileage, but the six leading companies operated 93 percent of the total mileage. In order of mileage, they were Wells Fargo, American Express, Adams, Southern Express, United States Express, and Pacific Express.

Mail was the railroads' highest-priority commodity for more than 100 years. Workers transfer mail between a truck and a Lehigh Valley Railway Post Office car around 1910. *Library of Congress*

Express evolution

The company that would eventually become Railway Express Agency was the ultimate maturation of the hundreds of express companies that led to the companies just listed. By 1906, the number of reporting express companies dropped to 14.

As an example, in 1907, 18 different railroads held stock in Adams Express, ranging from $6.1 million in shares by the Pennsylvania down to $2,100 by Boston & Providence. Adams claimed a total mileage of 34,900, of which railroad routes accounted for 30,700 miles. Railroads that didn't own shares of express companies had contracts with them for handling and transporting express.

These agreements generally specified the minimum rate the express company could charge for a shipment—specifically, that it could not be less than 150 percent of whatever the railroad's own LCL freight rate would be for the shipment (and the rate was usually 200 percent and sometimes as high as 300 percent). The railroad

then earned a specified percentage of the express payment for handling the shipment.

In addition, many express companies were related, holding shares in each others' companies. In 1907, Southern Express, for example, held stock in Adams Express, American Express, and United States Express, **5**.

The express companies controlled various routes and territories, using a combination of their own coaches (and eventually motor vehicles), railroad cars, and steamship lines. Some towns had offices of two or more express companies; other towns were "exclusive" and were served by only one company.

Shipments were regularly transferred among companies, just as with LCL freight handled directly by railroads. If, for example, a shipment would start at an Adams office but be delivered 1,000 miles away at a city exclusive to Western, the rate would be calculated in two parts: first to the farthest point Adams would carry it and then for the remaining mileage

from the transfer point to Western.

Two major blows to express companies came in 1913. First, the U.S. Post Office began accepting packages as it established Parcel Post (Fourth Class) service. This initially meant any package up to 11 pounds and sized no larger than a combined 72" (length + width + height), but the weight limit was gradually increased and reached 70 pounds by 1931.

Although generally a slower service, Parcel Post was also less expensive than express, and the service took a big bite out of the express business—especially for small personal packages. Express companies objected, protesting that Parcel Post was subsidized by the government (and operated at a loss) and thus amounted to unfair competition. This argument would last through REA's final days.

Second, express companies were found to be common carriers and subject to the Hepburn Act of 1906, meaning that companies couldn't simply set rates: they had to file their rate charges with the Interstate

5

Deliverymen offload a strongbox from an express truck in the 1910s. United States Express was one of 14 express companies still operating at the time. *Library of Congress*

Commerce Commission (ICC) and get ICC approval for any change in rates.

The result was another round of mergers and express companies going out of business. By the mid-1910s, the struggling express industry was down to four major interstate companies: Adams Express, American Express, Southern Express, and Wells Fargo; a surviving minor company, Western Express; and two railroad-owned companies: Great Northern Express and Northern Express (run by Northern Pacific).

As chapter 3 explains in detail, World War I saw the consolidation of these companies into a single entity: American Railway Express, which became Railway Express Agency in 1929. The amount of express traffic would decrease during the Depression through the 1930s but then see a resurgence during and immediately after World War II.

In the late 1940s, however, a rapid decline began as truck-based carriers—aided by larger, more-efficient trucks, improving roads, and the coming of Interstate highways—won increasing amounts of express and regular LCL traffic from REA and railroads.

Railway Express Agency was hampered by ICC restrictions and

regulations that forced it to use railcars instead of its own trucks for most long hauls, even as the number of passenger trains and routes diminished. Shipments dropped sharply in the 1960s, and after multiple attempts at reorganization and streamlining, REA declared bankruptcy and ceased operations in 1975.

Railroad LCL and mail

Railroads began carrying LCL parcels and cargo—also known as *break-bulk, merchandise,* or *package traffic*—from their beginnings in the early 1800s. This could mean small parcels, large cases or crates, barrels, or a collection of packages ranging from a few pounds to several tons. Shipments would be collected at local depots, forwarded to large freight houses or transfer terminals, unloaded and sorted, and then reloaded and forwarded to a transfer house close to the destination. The process was repeated until the shipment reached the local depot or freight house closest to the recipient, **6**.

Through the 1800s, this could be an especially time-consuming process. With hundreds of railroads in operation, there would be an almost infinite number of routing choices between two distant points. Cargo

would often have to be loaded and unloaded multiple times.

This process became more streamlined as small railroads merged to form larger systems and large railroads absorbed and bought smaller lines. As chapters 2 and 6 explain, by the early 1900s, railroads were building large freight houses in big cities and developing detailed car routing to both on-line points and other railroads' terminals. This made service faster and limited the number of times shipments required reloading.

Railroad LCL traffic peaked in 1929, when more than 13 million carloads were shipped. Even at that point, trucks were beginning to capture LCL shipments, especially for short hauls. The number of highway trucks registered in the United States rose from just over a million in 1920 to 3.4 million in 1929—a period that saw a slight decline in the number of freight cars in service. By that point, some railroads were estimating they had lost between 70 and 90 percent of LCL traffic for hauls of 100 miles or less and 25 percent of LCL traffic up to 200 miles. The mileage range of what was an economical trip for a truck at that point was about 200 to 250 miles, but that would expand quickly.

A Rutland local freight pauses to offload LCL packages from a peddler boxcar into the freight room at the Stephentown, N.Y., depot in 1953. *Jim Shaughnessy*

Even in the early 1920s, when trucks were just beginning to make inroads in freight traffic, it was widely recognized that trucks were more efficient than railroads for short-haul moves. For LCL, this was especially true for light-traffic branch lines and secondary lines, where railroads were losing money on the service.

By the 1920s, many railroads began operating trucks, either directly by establishing a subsidiary trucking company or by contracting with local drayage companies. Railroads (and trucks) were heavily regulated. They were limited by the ICC in exactly what trucking services they could provide. For the most part, it meant pickup and delivery of LCL and/or operating trucks to serve customers along their own rail routes and stations—using a tractor-trailer instead of a boxcar to deliver LCL to towns along a branch line, for example.

There were debates in the pages of the trade magazine *Railway Age*,

even as early as 1922, about whether railroads should continue in the LCL business at all or cede it all to trucks entirely—and this was when LCL still accounted for more than 12 million carloads annually. Many in the industry understood that trucks were here to stay and knew that they would continue to take business away from the railroads.

LCL traffic followed the trends of the express business, with carloadings dropping during the Depression but picking up immediately after World War II. LCL carloadings increased immediately after World War II, from 5.5 million in 1945 to 6.3 million in 1946, but it proved to be a temporary gain.

At that time, many railroads made a last effort to regain and maintain LCL traffic by starting named services aimed directly at merchandise shipments. These included Cotton Belt's *Blue Streak*, New York Central's *Pacemaker* service, Pennsylvania's Keystone service, and Southern

Pacific's *Overnight* trains, **7**. Many included new or rebuilt high-speed equipment, bright paint schemes, and dedicated LCL trains on expedited schedules.

However, none of these services could stem the tide of LCL traffic moving to trucks. By the 1950s, trucking companies could handle the traffic more efficiently. Trucks were large and efficient, roads were paved and well maintained, and the Interstate highway system was being developed. Trucks were easier to schedule, could readily adjust to traffic trends and new routes, and offered better delivery options. This was true even more for railroad LCL than express, as the duplication of railroad services (with more than 100 railroads offering this in the late 1940s) required more manpower and facilities compared to REA, which operated as a single entity.

The drop in LCL traffic (from 4.2 million carloads in 1950 to 1.8 million in 1960) meant the business, with its

Cotton Belt's *Blue Streak* merchandise train rolls through Texarkana, Texas, behind EMD FT diesels in 1949. *R. S. Plummer*

Some "passenger" trains existed primarily or exclusively to carry express and mail. In December 1949, a Burlington westbound mail express train rolls near Keenesburg, Colo., with an express boxcar (rebuilt troop car), RPO, two baggage express cars, another RPO, and a single rider coach in December 1949. *Joe Schick, Jim Seacrest collection*

high labor and facilities costs, was no longer profitable. In the 1950s, many railroads began increasing minimum weights for LCL shipments or dropped the service altogether. Merchandise traffic plummeted in the 1960s, and by 1970, LCL was essentially dead, with a mere 46,700 carloads shipped.

Demise of mail by rail

Mail by rail followed the fortunes of the passenger train. Mail routes were well established by the turn of the 20th century, and Railway Post Office cars (along with storage cars) covered almost every line in the country that handled passenger trains, from main and secondary lines to one-train-a-day branches, **8**.

The popularity of the automobile in the 1930s and 1940s, with the growth of air travel from the 1940s onward, caused a falloff in passenger numbers. This resulted in an ever-declining number of passenger trains and routes from the 1930s onward. Branch-line service was the first to go and followed by secondary routes.

The number of working RPO cars dropped significantly by the 1960s, but railroads still carried a great deal of storage mail, especially on major routes. That decade, however, saw railroads cut back dramatically on passenger trains. The U.S. Postal Service terminated most rail mail contracts in 1967, although a few routes lingered into Amtrak service. The last RPO route, on Amtrak from New York to Washington, D.C., made its last run in 1977.

Next, we'll begin an in-depth look at the facilities, operations, and equipment that provided these services, starting with railroad LCL services.

CHAPTER TWO

Railroad LCL traffic

In designing model railroads and planning model operations, we often focus on factories and industries that ship out entire carloads of products. However, into the 1960s, railroads handled a significant amount of packages, crates, and other shipments that didn't take up an entire boxcar. This is most commonly referred to as less-than-carload (LCL) traffic, and is also known as merchandise, package, and break-bulk freight, **1**.

New York Central's *Pacemaker* merchandise service debuted in 1946, with specially equipped and painted (vermillion and gray) boxcars—and the railroad even painted five cabooses for the service. *Pacemaker* trains originally operated from New York City to Buffalo, but the service was expanded in later years. *New York Central*

A variety of LCL goods are visible in this view of Kansas City Southern's New Orleans freight house in the 1940s, including cases of cigarettes and liquor, tires (wrapped), wire spools, and a variety of crated goods. *Leon Trice*

These shipments ranged from a single cardboard carton of cereal boxes that could be carried by hand to a crate containing a metal casting weighing a thousand pounds or a collection of boxes and crates weighing several tons, **2**.

From the early days of railroading through the 1940s, LCL shipments were a profitable business for railroads. An LCL car may contain a hundred smaller parcels that, in total, fill only half of the boxcar, **3**, but because each item is billed at a higher rate, that LCL car could generate several times the revenue compared to a carload rate. Specific LCL rates varied according to the type of shipment, with several rate classes based on the value of the commodity. Rates were per hundredweight (100 pounds or fraction thereof).

The tradeoff for this potentially higher revenue was that handling LCL traffic was extremely labor intensive. The service required thousands of employees, from local station agents to clerks, package handlers, dock workers, and drivers. Facility and operation

expenses were also high, with multiple freight houses and transfer terminals, all of which required extensive switching operations.

Consider that each railroad had its own LCL operation—and that there were more than 100 Class I railroads operating into the 1950s—and the enormous scale of merchandise operations and logistics comes into focus. There were 10,000 freight houses in service in the mid-1940s, ranging from buildings in small cities to large-city transfer terminals (more on those in chapter 5), plus more than 50,000 local combination depots that handled LCL shipments.

The other downside was that LCL shipments had high rates of damage and loss—much higher than carload freight. Each item was handled multiple times, increasing exposure, and rough handling from slack action and hard coupling could easily damage loose or improperly secured items. Damage claims were as high as 8 percent of LCL revenue in the 1920s.

Basic operations

To efficiently handle merchandise traffic, railroads used a system of local depots, small-city freight houses, and huge freight terminals and transfer houses. Along with this were thousands of boxcars—most nondescript, some specially painted and equipped—to consolidate these shipments and forward them to their destinations.

The basic mechanics of handling and shipping LCL are easy to understand. Individual boxes, crates, and packages are collected at small depots, local freight stations, or large terminals. They are shipped to the closest large freight transfer house and offloaded. There, shipments are combined for common destinations, reloaded in boxcars, and routed to large transfer stations near their destinations, **4**.

There, the process goes in reverse, as packages are unloaded, sorted, and reloaded for their final destinations, eventually arriving at a local freight station or depot, where shipments would be loaded on trucks for final delivery, **5**.

Merchandise boxcars carried a variety of cased and crated items. The large chest is a Speedbox, used by the Missouri Pacific to protect groups of small LCL items belonging to a single shipper. *Missouri Pacific*

Merchandise cars operated on regular schedules between terminals, usually on a daily basis, but sometimes on an every-other-day or tri-weekly schedule. As chapter 6 explains, these cars were scheduled like passenger trains, making their deliveries to match published schedules—railroads provided LCL customers with schedules promising delivery in a specific number of days.

Cars were routed from transfer houses to both on- and off-line destinations, as railroads worked with each other to avoid handling parcels any more than necessary. The more times a shipment had to be unloaded and reloaded, the slower the journey would be, the more labor required, and the more likelihood for damage (and the resulting damage claim).

Types of traffic

So what types of goods typically traveled in LCL shipments? Almost anything that didn't warrant the significantly higher prices of faster express shipping, which usually cost

about double standard merchandise rates. (The next chapter covers that thoroughly.)

The majority of LCL traffic comprised products traveling between businesses, or from distributors and manufacturers to retailers and other final customers—mainly manufactured goods, as opposed to raw materials. Examples include all types of groceries (cases of cans, bottles, jars, and packaged food products from soup to cereal), furniture, appliances, clothing, tools, paint, shoes, hardware, electric products, all manner of household goods, paper goods, and business supplies.

Especially through the 1940s, small and large retail stores of all kinds that were located away from large cities received much of their merchandise via LCL shipments. Shops in metro areas were often served by distributors and wholesalers who used their own delivery trucks—a service that gradually expanded to rural areas in the 1940s and later.

A small town in rural Iowa, for example, might have four grocery stores, two hardware stores, a clothing store, a variety store, and a shoe store—all of which would receive goods on a regular basis from their distributors via LCL, **6**. This is how even a small-town combination depot might rate a car or two of LCL per day.

Large mail-order companies, such as Montgomery Ward, Sears, and Spiegel, were major users of railroad LCL services. As chapter 6 explains, they would load multiple carloads of LCL packages at their distribution centers, which would be delivered to local railroad transfer stations and then be broken down for shipment to customers across the country.

Industrial customers would send small shipments of castings, machine parts, and other components via LCL. For example, multiple automobile engine blocks going to a manufacturing plant would be shipped by carload freight, but a single engine block going

LCL cars—including several Southern Pacific *Overnight* boxcars—are being loaded on parallel tracks at Pacific Electric's 8th Street Freight Station in Los Angeles. PE was an SP subsidiary. *Pacific Electric*

to a small-town automotive dealer would be shipped by LCL.

History

Railroads hauled LCL traffic since the establishment of the first rail lines in the country. Shipping LCL by rail was really the only option for businesses, other than horse-drawn wagons for short hauls and express shipments—at higher rates—for smaller parcels (more on that in chapter 3).

Railroads through the late 1800s were unregulated, and in essence were free to set whatever rates they thought the market would bear. This led to high charges in some areas where railroads had monopolies and widely varied charges in other areas. There was little consistency in rates, as there were still hundreds of small railroads across the country, with more being built. An LCL shipment might travel across several railroads, with each line wanting to get as much of the total charge as possible.

The first step toward regulating rates and services came in 1887 when Congress passed the Interstate Commerce Act, which established the Interstate Commerce Commission (ICC). The act directed the ICC to encourage competition and gave it the power to ban types of rate-setting it thought discriminatory or those that amounted to collusion among railroads.

The ICC gained more power in 1906 with the Hepburn Act, which allowed the ICC to hear complaints and adjust what it found to be unfair rates to ones it deemed "just and reasonable." By that time, there were fewer railroads as many small lines were acquired by larger railroads. Boxcars were increasing in size, and train length and speeds were increasing, which led to better and faster overall service for both LCL and carload freight. The system of freight houses and transfer stations was firmly established and was used by railroads throughout the country, and LCL traffic in terms of total

tonnage and carloadings continued to grow by World War I. However, the rate impositions of the Hepburn Act kept rates lower than what railroads needed to keep up with rising costs and inflation, and by the time the United States entered the war, many railroads were in financial trouble and several were in receivership.

Railroads struggled to cope with increased wartime traffic, and in December 1917, President Woodrow Wilson ordered the nationalization of the country's railroads under the United States Railroad Administration. Operations were streamlined among railroads, duplicate services were eliminated, and new equipment ordered.

The Transportation Act of 1920 (also known as the Esch-Cummins Act) returned the railroads to private control, although all express services remained consolidated as a unified monopoly coordinated among railroads (see chapter 3) as the American Railway Express Co. Standard LCL

Side-door cabooses were sometimes used for delivering LCL to branchline stations. This is at Chicopee, Mo., on the St. Louis-San Francisco. *Wayne Leeman*

service, however, returned to individual railroad control.

Esch-Cummins also gave the ICC broad powers to regulate railroad freight rates, fix minimum rates, and approve mergers and abandonments in service and routes. This would have far-reaching effects on railroads regarding LCL service, greatly limiting them regarding rates in a time when trucking companies were becoming serious competitors.

Railroads moved a lot of merchandise traffic at this time: 53 million tons in 1920 and 67 million tons in 1921. By the early 1930s, there were more than 10,000 regularly scheduled LCL moves between cities or terminals. However, trucks were already beginning to capture a lot of LCL business, especially short-haul business (under 100 miles). Total LCL tonnage began to drop, with total LCL carloadings peaking in 1929 at 13.3 million.

Depression and competition

From 1930 onward, merchandise traffic began to drop, partially because of the Depression and, in part, because trucks were taking more and more of the business that did still exist. Railroad LCL carloads fell to 8.1 million by 1935—only 61 percent of the traffic carried just six years earlier.

In the midst of this financial climate, railroads were trying to take

measures to save what was still lucrative business: in 1932, LCL accounted for just 2.4 percent of total tonnage hauled but 10 percent of total revenue.

A bold attempt came in 1931, when the St. Louis Southwestern (best known as the Cotton Belt) inaugurated an all-LCL train providing overnight service between East St. Louis and Pine Bluff, Ark., with connections to Shreveport, La., and Texarkana, Ark. Service included integrated truck delivery (provided by subsidiary Southwestern Transportation Co.). Packages received by 5:30 p.m. in St. Louis would be delivered to customers along the route the next morning, **7**.

Named the *Blue Streak*, the train was a radical move in the midst of a Depression, especially for a railroad teetering on bankruptcy. It was the first attempt at an all-LCL overnight train. It ran on a first-class schedule at passenger-train speed with passenger locomotives. Cars were set out at intermediate points, with trucks waiting to transfer and deliver shipments.

Other neighboring railroads vehemently protested the service, saying it was an unneeded, expensive service and waste of resources that—as competitors—they would be forced to match. However, the Cotton Belt pointed out that the *Blue Streak* wasn't competing against other railroads, but against

trucks, of which there were already several companies providing overnight service in that territory.

The first train ran with nine cars, but business gradually increased. In 1935, Cotton Belt extended the *Blue Streak* by providing second-morning service to Dallas and Fort Worth. Other railroads then began their own expedited LCL services, such as the New York Central's *Merchandiser*, begun between Buffalo and New York City in 1934, Southern Pacific's *Overnight* service between San Francisco and Los Angeles, which debuted in 1935, and Union Pacific's *Challenger* Merchandise Service, started in 1939 with special cars.

In 1935, Congress passed the Motor Carrier Act. This gave the ICC authority to regulate trucking companies operating in more than one state. The Act gave the ICC power to set rates (similar to what railroads were already dealing with) and the power to grant operating permits over specific routes.

This was a key, as a trucking company couldn't just begin offering common carrier service to new cities—it had to apply to operate over a new route. This had ramifications for railroads as well, as many operated trucks for LCL delivery. The ICC could define what specific trucking services railroads could and couldn't offer (and what rates

Several cases of Kellogg's cereal—fresh off a St. Louis Southwestern *Blue Streak* merchandise car—are loaded onto a subsidiary Southwestern Transportation truck for delivery to a local grocery store. *St. Louis Southwestern*

that could be charged), including piggyback service, which was in its infancy. Railway Express Agency would also be affected, and it was ICC regulations that kept REA from operating trucks as it needed which eventually contributed to that service's downfall.

Boom and bust for LCL

Carloadings for LCL actually increased in 1936 and 1937 as the country began climbing out of the Depression, but truck traffic was booming, and other than a brief spike in 1941, rail LCL numbers dropped from 1938 through World War II. Route mileage covered by intercity trucks increased 500 percent from 1925 to 1940, but trucking ton-miles increased 1,000 percent in that time.

World War II dramatically increased most types of rail traffic, while LCL held steady at 5.5 million carloads in 1945. Expedited LCL services had been interrupted by wartime traffic, but as the war ended, many railroads made a push to reclaim merchandise traffic lost to trucks (or at least retain existing traffic).

The *Blue Streak* continued on, expanding to Los Angeles over Cotton

Belt parent Southern Pacific as the *Blue Streak Merchandise*. SP resumed its *Overnight* service, which had been interrupted by the war, but Union Pacific's *Challenger* merchandise cars were repainted for express service.

Among the best known new services and trains were New York Central's *Pacemaker* service, launched with great fanfare with bright red-and-gray boxcars in 1946, Pennsylvania's Keystone service (1950), and Missouri Pacific's *Eagle* service (1951) with distinctive blue, gray, and yellow cars.

Along with fancy paint schemes, these services featured new and rebuilt equipment (more on that in chapter 4) including high-speed trucks and brake gear. Railroads touted their expedited schedules through ads in trade publications, promising improved handling and delivery times.

Tied to this was increased use of trucks for delivery and pickup, including piggyback service, **8**. As many small depots were being closed, railroads began using trucks to cover longer routes along their rail lines.

LCL traffic actually rose slightly in 1946 and 1947, but then began a rapid decline that improved equipment

and scheduling couldn't combat. For railroads, when the volume of parcels was high, the extensive railroad LCL system worked. However, trucks had taken over enough LCL traffic that revenue no longer covered the labor- and equipment-intensive service.

A big dent in railroad LCL traffic came from the growth of freight forwarders from the 1940s into the 1950s. Freight forwarders, or consolidators, solicited LCL traffic in one location, consolidated the shipments and paid carload (railroad) or truckload rates to the destination city, and then contracted for delivery locally at the destination.

This wasn't necessarily bad for railroads, as railroads still handled much of the business anyway but as carload freight. This was at a lower rate but without any of the trouble or overhead expenses of handling the LCL themselves. In fact, as forwarders obtained more traffic, they often rented space in railroad facilities—often in large freight houses where railroads no longer required extensive space for their dwindling merchandise services. And several forwarders were, in fact, subsidiaries of railroads (or of other railroad-owned

The first *Blue Streak* merchandise train rolls west of Mount Pleasant, Texas, behind a Ten-Wheeler on October 1, 1931. *Harold K. Vollrath collection*

Several delivery trucks are lined up at New York Central's Indianapolis freight station in the mid-1940s. The trucks carry the NYC herald on their cabs, but they are lettered for subsidiary Strohm Warehouse and Cartage. *New York Central*

subsidiaries). Examples were Universal Carloading & Distributing, controlled by NYC, and National Carloading Corp., owned by Santa Fe.

The thorn for railroads was that forwarders concentrated on heavy-volume routes between major cities—skimming the cream of the business—while leaving the railroads' own LCL services to handle less-profitable routes and destinations. This, along with rising labor costs, was what ultimately led railroads to leave the LCL business.

By 1950, LCL carloadings had dropped to 4.3 million, and by 1955, it was 3.2 million, and the writing was on the wall. Increased truck capacity—the

40-foot semitrailer was legal across the country by the late 1950s—and efficiency gave trucks flexibility that railroads simply couldn't match.

Duplicity in service was another factor, with 100-plus railroads offering LCL service into the 1950s. This was in sharp contrast to express traffic, which—although handled on most railroads—was operated by a single company, Railway Express Agency. Even that consolidation didn't help, as REA would last slightly longer before its demise in the 1970s.

A few railroads tried to hold on, with the Burlington Route opening a new large transfer station at Chicago (Cicero)

in 1955 and the Santa Fe opening a huge new freight house in Kansas City in 1961. However, the Chicago & North Western closed its huge Proviso freight house in 1960, as merchandise loads dropped to 1.8 million. That number would fall below a million in 1963, to 465,000 in 1965, and under 100,000 by 1969. By the end of the decade, the long history of railroad-provided less-than-carload service was done.

The plus side for railroads is that they still carry millions of tons of LCL (now LTL, for *less-than-load* or *less-than-truckload*)—it's just carried in the trailers and containers of companies such as Roadway, FedEx, and UPS.

Early LCL containers

An early effort to streamline LCL operations was New York Central's container service, operated by a subsidiary, the LCL Corporation. Developed in 1921, the operation represented one of the first true intermodal operations, with small shipping containers that could be loaded via crane aboard specially equipped gondolas and then transloaded to trailers that were trucked directly to shippers' docks. The appeal was that once parcels were loaded in containers, they were sealed, so parcels were not subject to damage and pilfering that could occur with repeated reloading.

The service started from Chicago to Cleveland and then branched to other routes. Pennsylvania saw opportunity as well, starting its own container LCL service (the Keystone Container Car Co.) in 1928. Pennsy's containers operated from New York to several cities including Philadelphia, Buffalo, and Cleveland.

The container services proved popular—especially among freight forwarders—mainly because users were charged a lower all-commodity rate instead of one of the standard rates that usually applied to LCL shipments, which were based on type and value of commodity. The NYC moved 10,000 containers in 1927 and more than 47,000 in 1930, and the Pennsy averaged more than 20,000 movements per year.

Highway and other rail competitors were not so impressed, however, and filed complaints with the ICC that the lower rate was unfair. In 1931, the ICC ruled that the railroads could indeed provide the service, but it forced them to raise rates. The NYC's container service faded away quickly, but the Pennsy continued operating containers (including bulk transport containers) for lower-rate items through the 1930s.

Container service would be attempted by Railway Express Agency and Canadian LCL and express companies in the 1960s and 1970s, but it would be double-stack trains of other companies' containers—and not railroad-operated LCL or express services—that would make container shipping viable by rail.

The New York Central experimented with containers for LCL shipments in the 1920s. The containers, in various sizes, required a crane to transfer them between gondolas and truck chassis. *New York Central*

LCL carloadings

Annual number of cars loaded with LCL freight on U.S. railroads

Year	Carloadings	Year	Carloadings	Year	Carloadings	Year	Carloadings	Year	Carloadings
1928	13,099,000	1937	8,458,000	1946	6,311,000	1955	3,230,000	1964	640,000
1929	13,270,000	1938	7,964,000	1947	6,072,000	1956	3,056,000	1965	465,000
1930	12,187,000	1939	7,843,000	1948	5,458,000	1957	2,750,000	1966	322,000
1931	10,950,000	1940	7,669,000	1949	4,600,000	1958	2,331,000	1967	242,000
1932	9,079,000	1941	8,042,000	1950	4,260,000	1959	2,100,000	1968	205,000
1933	8,428,000	1942	5,595,000	1951	3,752,000	1960	1,800,000	1969	96,000
1934	8,244,000	1943	5,080,000	1952	3,573,000	1961	1,450,000	1970	46,700
1935	8,134,000	1944	5,460,000	1953	3,503,000	1962	1,160,000	1971	28,300
1936	8,221,000	1945	5,526,000	1954	3,196,000	1963	868,000		

Statistics are collected from *Railway Age*, statistical review issues (generally the first, second, or third issue in January of each year).

CHAPTER THREE

Railway Express Agency

From the 1920s through the 1960s, Railway Express Agency, or REA, was synonymous with express. In the days before UPS and FedEx cornered the market on small parcel shipping, REA used the nation's railroads and its own huge fleet of familiar green delivery trucks to get parcels and other less-than-carload express items to businesses and individuals, **1**.

A Railway Express Agency truck is backed up to the messenger car on Grand Trunk Western train 54 at Pontiac, Mich., to transfer express parcels in August 1956. Through the 1960s, it was REA's green trucks—not the brown ones of UPS—that America associated with package delivery service. *J. J. Buckley, Dan Pope collection*

What is express?

Express traffic was handled separately from standard less-than-carload (LCL) parcels and freight—in particular, express was handled by passenger trains, not freight trains. But what, exactly, set express shipments apart?

Express can be anything that requires expedited shipping, fast delivery, or special care in transit. A new toaster ordered from the Montgomery Ward catalog by a woman in Minot, N.D., in 1939 can be sent via standard freight, but if her old toaster was broken and she wanted toast immediately, that new toaster would travel by express.

Express commanded higher fees than standard LCL (typically twice the rate) and carried a minimum charge per package that usually priced it above its chief competitor, the U.S. Postal Service's Parcel Post.

From its inception in 1929, REA became known for taking on virtually any shipment presented to it, from live animals to machinery. At a time when eight days was about as fast as railroad LCL service could get items from coast to coast, REA promised delivery to almost anywhere in the United States in five days or less (faster when using the company's Air Express service) and had a reputation for coming through. REA also provided pickup as well as delivery service, so unlike Parcel Post you didn't have to lug your packages to the post office.

Grandma Mabel in Fresno needs to send Christmas presents to her grandkids in Virginia, Arkansas, and Georgia—call REA (and ask for the company's special "Do Not Open Until Christmas" labels).

A machine in a Los Angeles factory breaks down and needs a replacement part from a company in Cleveland—call REA (and probably specify Air Express).

A hatchery near Minneapolis needs to send 20 crates, each with 100 live baby chicks, to 10 different farmers in western South Dakota—call REA.

The variety of items that was shipped via REA is truly staggering. The company was best known among the public as the package delivery people,

2 Movie studios were prime customers of REA. Here, a vehicleman picks up a stack of scripts at Paramount in 1937. *Railway Express Agency*

3 Most REA agencies had offices in local railroad depots and shared freight room space. A safe in each office held cash and valuables. This is San Augustine, Texas, in 1939. *Russell Lee, Library of Congress*

like UPS today. If you had a parcel—such as a Christmas present—you could either drop it off at the office (almost always at the local railroad depot) or you call the office and a green truck would shortly stop by and pick it up.

The huge mail-order companies (such as Sears and Montgomery Ward) that, by the early 1900s, became especially popular with folks in rural areas were big customers of REA as well as the railroads' conventional LCL services. For the fastest delivery, customers could pay a premium to have their items shipped REA.

Although almost invisible to the general public, the biggest customers of REA were industries and businesses that shipped machinery, parts, and goods in a business-to-business environment. Business owners knew well that time is money, and saving days in transit time was often worth the cost for expedited shipping.

Motion pictures were shipped by REA. Film was fragile, flammable, sensitive to heat and humidity, and required careful handling. Initial releases were often shipped via Air Express to big-city theaters around the country. A weekly ritual for REA agents and drivers was picking up films from theaters in larger towns and prepping them for shipment to the next smaller town down the line—a process repeated as each film progressed week by week from big-city premiere to small-city main feature to small-town second feature.

Movie and recording studios also used REA for many other items, including scripts, costumes, props, advertising and publicity materials, and music and sound recordings, 2.

Medical equipment often traveled via express. An REA news release in 1950 noted that the company shipped baby incubators about 10,000 times per year (often via air as well as rail) among hospitals.

Sports equipment was another express category. Louisville Slugger shipped thousands of wood bats each year to professional baseball teams, often via express. Pro and college teams would often have equipment and uniforms delivered by REA.

REA transported many live animals, including racehorses. Here, in April 1938, Seabiscuit (with his owner and trainer) is about to embark on a 4-day, 10-hour journey from California to New York in a Southern Pacific baggage car with portable stalls. *Railway Express Agency*

Cases of baby chicks were often shipped via REA. Here, several cases are being loaded aboard a streamlined baggage express car in 1937. *Railway Express Agency*

An REA step van delivers air express packages directly on the tarmac to a waiting American Airlines 707 in the early 1960s. *Railway Express Agency*

Cases of strawberries are transferred from pickup trucks to a National Refrigerator Car express reefer at Hammond, La., in 1939. REA handled LCL and carload lots of refrigerated express in its own cars as well as railroad-owned cars. *Russell Lee, Library of Congress*

Fish and seafood often traveled by express. Here, fresh shrimp in insulated, foam-lined cases is loaded aboard a standard baggage express car at Biloxi, Miss. *Goodyear*

Valuables, including jewelry, precious metals, negotiated checks, bonds, and cash, were frequently shipped via REA. The U.S. government was a major customer for this, as Federal Reserve Banks used REA to send cash among branches, and the government sent cash to military bases for payroll. A safe in the REA messenger's baggage car served as the repository. REA agencies in depots had safes to store valuables, **3**, while large terminals had a "value room" for cash and valuables, with armed guards on duty. Larger shipments of gold, silver, and ore would have multiple armed guards and messengers.

Baggage was also common, but not the checked baggage of train passengers. This could include trunks and suitcases forwarded to colleges ahead of students as the school year started; belongings to and from military bases as soldiers were transferred, inducted, or discharged; families forwarding trunks to resorts or vacation destinations; or cases and household goods for a family that was moving.

Live animals were accepted for express shipments, especially high-value breeding stock. Racehorses are an example of a high-value animal often shipped, and REA handled almost all traffic among racetracks, especially in the Northeast and Midwest, **4**. They would be carried in a horse car (usually rented from a railroad) or a baggage car equipped with portable stalls and having special attendants.

Pets, such as dogs or cats, and other small animals could be caged and crated and shipped in standard baggage cars. Such shipments required that food and water be supplied, and would include special handling instructions for the messengers and agents, such as feeding and walking.

Baby chicks were sent by the millions via REA from hatcheries to farmers in rural areas, as they could survive for three days in their boxes without additional food or water, **5**. In 1940, a single hatchery in Indiana sent more than a million chicks via express. Turkeys and other birds were other common shipments.

Zoo animals and other exotic animals would also be handled, often in special shipments. REA was not shy about publicizing any of these shipments via ads, news releases, and photos, and its own employee magazine (*The Express Messenger*) often had stories and details of exotic shipments.

In areas that didn't warrant full milk car or milk train service, REA handled milk and cream cans among stations. These were carried in standard baggage (messenger) cars, and depending upon the weather, might require the messenger to keep ice atop the cans to keep the contents from spoiling.

The military provided shipments—including many top-secret moves, such as equipment and atomic "fissionable materials" traveling in customized lead-lined cars via REA (more on these cars in chapter 4).

Other shipments included furniture, appliances, various food products, almost any type of consumer goods, fresh eggs, clothing, human remains in caskets, and high-priority paperwork (financial forms, contracts, deeds, stocks and bonds).

Air express warranted a premium price, but enabled same-day or overnight delivery in many cases—a radical development for the 1930s and '40s, **6**. Items traveling by air included newsreels, news photos, and other film; recordings for radio; machinery and parts; financial documents and canceled checks; flowers (especially at Easter and Christmas); and human blood. About the only things not accepted for air shipment were livestock, explosives, or "iced goods" (those that required re-icing in transit).

Refrigerated express

REA also handled items that required refrigeration. REA and various railroads had fleets of ice-bunker express refrigerator cars equipped to travel in passenger trains (see chapter 4 for details).

Shippers were willing to pay express rates for items that were very perishable. Most berries, for example, had short shelf lives, and were almost always shipped by express, **7**. Express

Church containers were wheeled, insulated chests that could carry a small refrigerated load and either water or dry ice. They were easily loaded on trucks or railcars. *Railway Express Agency*

REA started REA Leasing Corp. (Realco) in the early 1960s, selling the division at a profit in 1969. This cryogenic trailer was new in 1961. *Railway Express Agency*

rates were also paid for high-demand products, such as the first fruits produced in a given growing season or region, or those products known for being the best of their type. Other perishables requiring refrigeration that traveled in express reefers included cut flowers; many types of plants, including strawberry and tomato; prepacked gift baskets and packages of fruit, meat, and cheese; and fresh fish and seafood.

Dressed game animals (or the meat from them) were often sent home from hunting trips via REA.

Many refrigerated items traveled in standard cars as well. Shippers could pack products such as fresh fish or seafood in sealed containers with insulation and dry ice, **8**. Another option, developed in the mid-1930s, was placing small lots of perishables in REA-supplied insulated rolling chests called *Church containers*, **9**.

Church containers (named for their inventor, Major Elihu Church) look like large chests or trunks with rolling casters, making them reasonably easy to move. They have a galvanized steel

In the early 1960s, REA experimented with containers with built-in stands that could be carried on short delivery truck chassis and semitrailer chassis. *REA Express*

shell, 4" of insulation, a pocket for ice or dry ice to keep the interior cool, and a 10-cubic-foot capacity. The REA had about 500 of them in service before World War II (1,000 by 1950), and they could be transported in trucks, in baggage cars, or by air.

These containers were popular for produce, fish, and seafood, as they could keep their contents at a constant temperature for up to four days. An REA truck would deliver a container to a shipper's place of business. The shipper would load the container and seal it, and a truck would pick it up and bring it to the depot, where it would be transferred to a railcar. The container would be handled like any other shipment, remaining sealed until delivery to the customer.

Church containers gained some fame for their inventor and REA during World War II, as they proved to be ideal for transporting pints of donated blood—a commodity for which temperature control was critical.

The blood was collected and packed by the Red Cross and shipped by REA in Church containers from donor centers to laboratories, where plasma was extracted for shipping overseas. During the war, almost all Church containers in service were dedicated to that use.

History of REA

As the United States entered World War I in 1917, the country's railroads struggled to keep up with the tremendous increases in traffic. In particular, railroads were not cooperating when it came to efficiently moving freight via interchange: competition was taking preference over cooperation. This was accentuated by the fact that there were still hundreds of railroads fighting for traffic.

As a result, in December 1917, President Woodrow Wilson ordered that U.S. railroads be taken over by a national body, the United States Railroad Administration (USRA). Railroads were organized by regions,

new equipment was ordered, duplicate operations and facilities were eliminated, and operations were streamlined. After the war ended, control was restored to individual railroads in March 1920.

At the time the USRA gained control of railroads, the seven surviving express companies were combined as well, under the name American Railway Express Co. (ARE). Duplicate offices were closed, small offices and agencies were combined, uniform nationwide billing was adopted, equipment was pooled, and operations were streamlined as much as possible.

Following the war, the intent was to divide ARE back into its original companies, but the nature of changes and operations during the war made this impossible. Unlike railroads, which had the physical plant of rails in given routes, the express companies only had their services. Because of the consolidation of agencies and equipment, there was no way to

Milwaukee's Key-Point REA Terminal, opened in 1962, eliminated several smaller agencies. Vans and straight trucks were for local delivery and pickup, while semis connected with other regional terminals. *REA Express*

accurately define who had what, so American Railway Express continued on as an entity. An exception was Southeastern Express, which was formed to cover the Southern Railway and connecting short lines.

Railway Express Agency was created in 1929 when 86 Class I railroads purchased the assets of American Railway Express (according to an option in their 1920 contracts signed with ARE). The railroads divided ownership shares based on the amount of express traffic they carried, signing a 25-year contract with REA. Southeastern Express remained a holdout at that time, and remained independent until 1938, when it was acquired by REA. Non-owning railroads were still allowed to participate in REA service but would not share in profits.

The agreement gave REA the exclusive right to handle express shipments on U.S. rail lines, with railroads providing equipment (space

In 1970, REA adopted a new paint scheme on trucks, going from green to light gray and blue, and replaced the diamond herald with an arrow. *Russ MacNeil collection*

on passenger trains in the form of baggage cars), moving the trains, and providing terminal space (generally in railroad depots), while REA handled all pickup, delivery, and transfer of parcels, as well as billing and management.

Profits beyond REA operating costs would be distributed to the owning railroads based proportionately on the amount of shipments on each carrier. The tradeoff for having a monopoly in place was extensive regulation regarding rates, which came from the ICC.

An REA truck (right) and mail messenger's pickup truck (left) meet the Des Moines to Washington, Iowa, local at Oskaloosa, Iowa, in March 1948. *Robert Milner*

An expressman driving a "mule" pulls three carts of outbound express into position along the platform at Centralia, Ill., in July 1946. *Henry McCord*

Part of the agreement stipulated that REA would distribute traffic among owning railroads equitably (since many major cities were joined by two or more owning railroads). A key point was that REA could use trucks or airplanes to carry express shipments **only** with the consent of the railroad(s) that would have participated in the shipment.

Express traffic increased in the late 1930s as the country eased out of the Depression, and it was stable through and immediately after World War II. After that time, however, REA began to see increased competition from truck lines. Along with that, passenger-train miles dropped, as automobiles and airplanes took more and more people away from rail travel. This began to limit the efficiency of shipping to many locations by rail.

Unlike its trucking company competitors, REA was hamstrung by having to use rail lines for all routes that had passenger service. It could not simply substitute trucks along a rail-served route without an agreement from the railroads. And even when that permission was granted, REA trucks were limited to traveling on that exact route.

A key point to remember is that in that era, railroads and trucking lines were both heavily regulated by the ICC. New trucking routes could not simply be started (by REA or a trucking firm) without ICC approval, and trucking companies were quick to lodge protests at any expansion of REA truck operations that the truckers considered to be competitive to their services.

REA still fared well through the 1940s and into the 1950s, even contributing slightly more revenues to railroads in 1953 than it had in 1944. However, this was due to an increase in rates. The actual volume of traffic was dropping dramatically: 77 million shipments in 1954 compared to 231 million in 1946 and 110 million in 1949.

By the late 1950s, revenues from express traffic were dropping along with total shipments. As with railroad LTL service, REA was hurt by improved roads, the new Interstate highway system, and increased truck sizes. It was obvious that REA's original business model was not sustainable, and the agreements between REA and the railroads were changed to reflect that.

Starting in 1961, REA gained permission to use trucks on any of its routes as needed. How it reimbursed railroads also changed. Instead of railroads simply providing space in cars, REA began leasing space in railroad cars on an as-needed basis and dividing the revenue from each shipment with the carrying railroad.

The new agreement made REA profitable again for a period in the early 1960s, and actually saw a slight increase in shipments from 1962 to 1963 (59 million to 59.8 million). REA tried to emphasize its air express service, which

Several express parcels are being loaded aboard a Gulf, Mobile & Ohio gas-electric in the late 1950s. *Paul Larson*

An expressmen and messenger sort and unload express parcels at Fonda, N.Y., on the Fonda, Johnstown & Gloversville in the late 1950s. *Jim Shaughnessy*

A Railway Express truck exchanges parcels with a St. Louis Southwestern gas-electric in the 1940s. *Charles M. Mizell Jr.*

(since the late 1920s) it had operated in conjunction with various air carriers. It also started Realco (REA Leasing Co.), a national trailer-leasing pool, **10**, and experimented with piggyback and truck-rail container service to increase efficiency, **11**. The container system was called COST-KUT (Containers On Semi Trailers for Keypoint Unit Trucks), and was not as successful as hoped.

As part of its streamlining, REA also eliminated many small agencies, cutting 11,600 local offices in 1959 to 8,900 by 1963. The company opened more than 50 medium-sized distribution centers that it termed "key-point terminals," **12**. These served as hubs for both truck and rail operations and as bases for longer delivery-truck routes, which served the smaller agencies that had been closed. The idea was that sending out dozens of delivery trucks from one key-point terminal was more efficient than one or two trucks dispatched from dozens of small agencies (also see photo 28 on page 68).

However, total shipments and revenues continued to decline as shippers continued turning to truck carriers. By the early 1960s, motor carriers handled about 85 percent of intercity LCL traffic (compared to about 5 percent for railroads' non-express traffic and 2 percent for REA).

Declining passenger trains hampered the "rail-haul" clause of REA shipping by truck. In many cases, REA wasn't allowed to handle parcels between two cities by truck unless they had traveled (or would subsequently travel) by rail. The trucking companies gaining this traffic were not bound by such rules.

United Parcel Service, for example, which began as a parcel delivery service in New York City, from the 1940s through the 1950s, gradually acquired truck routes nationwide. The company earned common-carrier status and the ability to carry LCL virtually anywhere in the country. UPS was able to schedule its trucks as needed, with no ties to train routes

or schedules, making it much more efficient that REA.

REA's Realco venture was actually successful: 66 railroads were members by 1964. However, Realco didn't do enough for actual REA operations, so Realco was sold (albeit for profit) to Integrated Container Services in 1969.

As passenger trains continued to be dropped, railroads began dropping out of the express business—which they were allowed to do, per the REA contract, with 18 months' notice. The Southern, Reading, New York Central, and others all did this, further hampering REA. The coming of Amtrak in 1971 eliminated most remaining passenger routes.

With its early 1960s changes, the company had changed its corporate image, calling itself REA Express, de-emphasizing the *Railway* part of the name as being archaic (and altering its diamond logo to REA initials over a large X.) In 1970, the company name was officially changed to REA Express, and the familiar diamond

The Railway Express Agency terminal in Chicago was adjacent to Union Station. Here, a Burlington Route switcher moves a pair of baggage express cars and an express boxcar between the terminal and station. *Louis A. Marre collection*

logo and green scheme on trucks were eliminated, replaced by light gray with an upward-pointing blue arrow, **13**.

A new ownership group comprising five of REA's corporate officers purchased REA in 1969, but the company's days were numbered. At the time, only 10 percent of REA revenues came from rail operations (compared to 60 percent from trucking and 25 percent from air), and the ICC estimated that REA handled less than 1 percent of intercity package traffic.

The new leadership terminated 4,000 employees, including half the company's vice presidents, and tried to further streamline operations. However, REA Express was doomed by the growth of UPS and LCL trucking lines, the drop in rail services, and ICC regulations. REA's shipments in 1972 were just half of what was shipped in 1965. Another blow came in 1974 with the Civil Aeronautics Board's order to airlines to drop REA's exclusive air express contracts.

REA Express declared bankruptcy in early 1975, amid litigation with UPS, its former owning railroads, the railway clerks' union, and other groups. Several executives would later be indicted on embezzlement and other charges. The company had hoped for reorganization, but it was not to be, and by late 1975, the courts ordered all operations terminated. REA came to an inglorious end in November of that year when courts ordered REA's assets to be liquidated, ending the long run of an American institution.

Basic operations

In its heyday, REA had more than 22,000 offices (or agencies), almost all located in local railroad stations. Those, plus large transfer terminals in big cities, together with the passenger trains of 100-plus railroads that traveled along 190,000 miles of track, allowed the company to carry shipments to all but the most rural outposts in the United States.

REA's overall organizational structure and operations were similar to the railroads' own LCL services, but—although using the trains, baggage cars, and facilities of those railroads—REA was run as a separate company, with its own employees responsible for the company's operations.

Let's look at the day-to-day operations of REA, starting with how a local agency went about its business.

Most agencies were based in local railroad stations, although some were in storefront buildings, **14**. REA's red diamond herald was a familiar sight, hanging on the ends of most local depots. Each agency had an established area for delivery. REA regularly published state-by-state lists of non-served towns, with references to which active agency should receive parcels for the non-served town. If a package came in for an address that was outside of the delivery area, a card would be filled out and sent to the recipient advising that the parcel was ready for pickup.

Several trucks are lined up for loading and unloading at the REA terminal in Louisville, Ky., adjacent to the Union Station, in 1960. *Louisville & Nashville*

Express refrigerator cars were often used for standard (nonrefrigerated) shipments. Here, express parcels are being loaded aboard an REA converted troop car/reefer in the early 1960s. *Paul Maximuke*

The smallest agencies, typically in small towns serving largely rural areas, were one-man operations. A single agent performed all tasks, including preparing paperwork, driving the truck to make pickups and deliveries, and getting parcels loaded and unloaded from trains.

Larger towns with more traffic would have multiple employees. An agent oversaw the operations; depending upon traffic volume, the office could have a separate cashier as well. The agent earned a commission on all originating shipments—this was done to encourage local agents to solicit and encourage new business.

One or more deliverymen (also called *vehiclemen*) would be employed to head out in their green trucks, making deliveries in the morning and pickups in the afternoon. Businesses would hang a small red diamond sign in a window or outside to alert drivers that a pickup was needed; businesses and individuals could also drop packages off or call to request a pickup.

An additional employee or two may be on hand to assist with waybills, labels, and paperwork and help load and unload railcars and trucks. Depending upon the size of the office and traffic levels, local agencies would sometimes have agreements allowing railroad employees or station agents to load and unload parcels from trains and perform other duties. REA was also contracted by railroads to perform

Railway Express staged this photo just before Easter in 1940 to highlight a shipment of 440 packages of flowers heading from San Francisco to the Midwest. *Railway Express Agency*

REA touted the door-to-door service of its air express, as opposed to airlines' own services, which only provided airport-to-airport service. *Railway Express Agency*

LCL pickup and delivery service in more than 1,000 locations and to perform baggage pickup and delivery as well.

Parcels collected for outbound shipping needed to have labels attached, a waybill filled out (in duplicate, one for each item being shipped), and any other necessary forms (special instructions for shipping, additional insurance, etc.) completed. Parcels could be shipped prepaid or collect-on-delivery (COD).

As a passenger train rolled in, one or more employees were waiting with carts or a truck to transfer inbound and outbound shipments, **15** and **16**. As chapter 6 explains, on routes with multiple passenger trains operating, specific trains would be assigned to serve stations on each route. For example, a station that saw eight trains a day likely wouldn't have express to transfer with every train.

The REA messenger aboard a baggage car would trade waybills with the local agent, **17**. The messenger would take charge of any valuables (such as shipments of currency or jewelry) and sign any necessary

transfer paperwork. Local agencies also transferred incoming company money (such as payments for shipments) to messengers, generally with the last available train of the day.

Messengers were assigned to specific trains, and rode in messenger cars (see chapter 4), which were baggage express cars outfitted with a desk, toilet, drinking water, lights, heat, and a safe. The messenger's job was to oversee the transfer of shipments at all the agencies served by that train.

Special duties included handling and guarding valuables, handling

24 A 1930s Ford REA truck is parked at the Kansas, Oklahoma & Gulf station at Henryetta, Okla., in 1940. *Louis A. Marre collection*

25 A new mid-1930s International C-series REA truck displays a Sunkist advertising sign as it poses for the company photographer. *Railway Express Agency*

company cash and paperwork, and taking care of special requirements with shipments. This could include placing ice atop milk cans or feeding crated animals in transit.

Incoming parcels could be placed on carts and taken into the express area of the freight room and sorted for delivery; they could also be loaded directly onto a truck, **18**.

Once a train arrived at its terminal (or large intermediate transfer station), workers with carts would meet the train to unload the express car or cars. At large cities, cars would be switched directly to tracks at the REA building, which in most cities was located adjacent to the station, **19** and **20** (more on that, as well as train operations, in chapter 5; also see photos 25 on page 66 and 26 on page 67). Teams of workers emptied the cars and sorted the incoming parcels based on their ultimate destinations.

At the same time, outbound cars were being prepared, based on individual train departure times. These could be sealed cars, with all the parcels heading to a distant point, or a messenger car, with items that would be distributed to agencies along the route of the train. Sealed cars would have an REA placard next to the door, indicating the origination, destination, car number, and any special instructions.

Sealed express cars—like cars of LCL or mail (chapter 7)—ran on regular schedules among REA terminals throughout the country. This was most often in baggage express or express boxcars, but express reefers were often used for standard (nonrefrigerated) express, **21**.

Air express

American Railway Express began air express operations in 1927, and the service was continued and expanded by REA, **22**. The company had a uniform contract with multiple airlines (most airlines that carried both passengers and cargo), which was approved by the Civil Aeronautics Board. The arrangement stipulated that REA performed all duties, including billing, except for actually loading and unloading (and flying) the planes.

The service allowed next-day delivery in many cases (and sometimes same-day delivery), an innovative concept in the 1930s and '40s. For this speed, air express commanded premium rates—often 10 times the standard express rate. This charge dropped over the years as airplanes became faster and more efficient. As an example, shipping a 25-pound box coast to coast via Air Express was $65 in 1927 (a trip that took 36 hours with 16 refueling stops) but only $21 in 1943 (a 16-hour, mainly overnight trip).

The profit from each air express shipment (billed amount less expenses) was divided between the carrying airline and REA (initially 75 percent for the airline and 25 percent for REA; this was changed to 87.5/12.5 in 1932). REA's profit was divided by the railroads.

For air service, REA performed pickup and delivery as with other express, using its trucks to either bring shipments directly to a local airport or using truck and rail to the nearest airport, **23**. This distinguished REA from airlines' own air cargo services, which only provided airport-to-airport service (instead of door-to-door or dock-to-dock).

As promotional photos often show, the usual practice was for REA trucks to deliver shipments directly to planes on the tarmac (and vice versa for pickups). As of 1940, REA's contract covered 17 airlines at 216 airports, and about 35 percent of air express shipments traveled in part by rail.

Air express was a small but significant portion of REA's business, and one the company tried to grow. REA handled 715,000 air shipments in 1935. This grew to 1.1 million in 1940 and 1.4 million in 1942; by 1962, it was 7.5 million. REA also provided international shipping via its partnership with Pan American Airways.

By REA's demise, air express accounted for about a quarter if its total revenues. It was, however, facing competition from a new breed of companies, including Federal Express.

REA's cowl-style trucks, with the cab integral to the body and sliding side doors, were common through the 1960s. Ida Hicks was one of several women employed as expressmen during World War II. This is New Britain, Conn., in 1943. *Gordon Parks, Library of Congress*

An early step van backs up to an express car on the Boston & Maine at North Bennington, Vt., in October 1947. These had high floors (above wheel level) and no lower body cowling. *Gene Baxter*

Trucks

Through the 1960s, REA was known for its extensive fleet of trucks wearing the company's distinctive green paint scheme with red wheels, red diamond herald, gold RAILWAY EXPRESS AGENCY lettering, and eye-catching advertising posters that graced the sides of the vehicles. The REA truck fleet was varied, with step vans, box trucks, and tractor-trailers of several manufacturers all performing various duties.

By the time World War I ended, the era of horse-and-wagon cartage was largely gone. At its formation in 1929, REA inherited American Railway Express's trucks and began adding great numbers of its own vehicles. The company operated about 12,000 vehicles by 1940 and 15,000 in 1953.

Early vehicles included open-cab designs with solid tires, Walker electric trucks (especially in New York City), and then in the 1930s, box bodies on conventional enclosed cab-and-chassis trucks from many builders, including Chevrolet, Diamond T, Ford,

By the mid-1950s, delivery vans took on a more modern look, with lowered body and full contoured cowling at the rear and front. The scheme was still green with gold lettering and red wheels. *Railway Express Agency*

A White tractor with box trailer and a Ford C-series cabover delivery truck wait at the dock at the Nashville REA terminal in the early 1960s. *REA Express*

International, Mack, Studebaker, and White, **24** and **25** (and photo 3 on page 6.

The integrated cowl-style cab and body delivery truck became an REA trademark, **18** and **26**. These early, distinctive trucks had the cab as the forward part of the box, but with a conventional hood protruding outward at the front. They allowed the driver to access parcels in the truck without having to exit the truck, walk to the rear, and open the door, which represented a significant time savings when picking up and delivering small parcels. These trucks were built atop chassis from many manufacturers. Versions were built from the 1930s into the 1950s, and they could be found in service through the 1960s.

The step-side van (tall panel truck) proved to be the ultimate vehicle for pickup and delivery routes. The precursers to these, built around 1940, had straight lower frames and flat interior floors above the wheel height, requiring a big step down when exiting the vehicle, **27**.

These led to the true step vans of the '50s, with a lower frame, lower doors, and fenders and cowling around the wheels, **28**. They became REA's standard delivery truck from the mid-1950s through the demise of the company in the 1970s.

Truck sizes and the number of trucks at each agency varied by need. A remote one-man agency might have a single cowl-style truck, a small agency might have one step van and one straight truck, and an agency in a large town or small city would have a few step vans and cowl trucks and a larger straight truck or two to serve larger businesses and industries.

REA also operated a variety of tractor-trailers, **29**. These were generally used in cities having multiple depots for making transfers, for large shipments, and on routes where trucks had replaced rail service. As with conventional trucks, these were from a variety of manufacturers and in several styles.

The large advertising banners found on the sides of REA trucks represented a significant source of income for the

Changing the paper signs on the sides of REA trucks was a monthly ritual. Klink Garrett pastes a new sign on the truck at a one-man agency in Wyoming around 1950. *Courtesy Toby Smith*

A pair of new International delivery vans are delivered via flatcar in 1958. The van at left carries AIR EXPRESS DIVISION lettering. *J. David Ingles collection*

company. Subjects included cigarettes, candy, gum, and many food products, as well as banners for Railway Express itself and its services. World War II saw a variety of banners imploring people to buy war bonds, as well as patriotic war-effort-themed ads.

A ritual took place around the first of each month when new 4 x 10-foot paper banners arrived at local agencies. The old banners would be scraped off the truck sides, and the new ones glued in place with water-based paste, **30**.

Truck lettering variations included vehicles with AIR EXPRESS lettering, **31**,

and some tractor-trailers in route service had RAILWAY EXPRESS MOTOR TRANSPORT lettering.

The corporate rebranding of 1960 led to changes in vehicle paint schemes. Lettering went from serif to a sans-serif style, now stating REA EXPRESS instead of the full company name. The paint was changed to a lighter green (termed *apple green*), and the new diamond logo (with REA initials over a white X) was used.

The final scheme, when the company officially became REA Express, was light gray with the new upward-pointing

REA used piggyback trailers in the Northeast in the early 1960s. This is the first run of New York-Chicago operations on Erie Lackawanna in March 1961. The flatcar is equipped with steam and signal lines for head-end operation. *REA Express*

diagonal arrow logo, introduced in 1970, with no more side advertising panels. The scheme debuted on 400 new International step vans delivered that year and on many trailers. Some additional older vehicles were repainted, but this scheme was not applied to all vehicles by the end of REA in 1975, and photos of trucks in this scheme are rare.

In the early 1960s, REA made a push for containerization, using a variety of standardized containers that could be easily transferred from straight trucks to semis to railcars and could also stand on their own.

Piggyback operations included trailers between New York and Boston on the New Haven (begun in 1958) and between Chicago and Philadelphia using Pennsylvania's TrucTrain piggyback service (starting in 1959), **32**. REA also shipped express in New York Central Flexi-Vans between Chicago, Detroit, and other Michigan cities, and in Chesapeake & Ohio's pioneering Railvan trailers (see chapter 7), also in Michigan service.

Chapter 4 shows examples of the baggage express cars and express refrigerator cars used by REA, and chapters 6 and 7 discuss express and mail train operations.

More Information

Two books deserve special mention if you're interested in modeling REA and its operations or are interested in the company's history. The first is *Railway Express: An Overview*, by V. S. Roseman, published in 1992 by Rocky Mountain Publishing (then the publisher of *Model Railroading* magazine). The book takes an in-depth look at REA, with lots of photos, data, and information on facilities, trucks, railcars, air express, and operations. It also includes a copy of REA's 1954 operating agreement with the railroads. In all, it's a great reference for Railway Express Agency.

The other book is *Ten Turtles to Tucumcari*, published in 2003 by University of New Mexico Press. The author is Klink Garrett, who started with REA in the late 1930s as an agent's assistant and worked many other positions, including deliveryman, cashier, agent, and messenger, eventually becoming an executive with the company and dealing with U.S. government shipments. Garrett wrote the book with Toby Smith, and they do a fine job of telling stories and explaining the day-to-day operations of an agency from the viewpoint of an agent, a driver, and a messenger.

Both books are out of print but copies can be found in libraries or online through abebooks.com, amazon.com, eBay, and other sources.

CHAPTER FOUR

Head-end cars and merchandise equipment

Mail and express parcels were carried in cars at the front of passenger trains—thus the term *head-end traffic*, **1**. This business was of course carried in head-end cars, which could mean baggage cars, express boxcars, and express refrigerator (reefer) cars. A railroad's own merchandise (nonexpress) less-than-carload (LCL) traffic rode in standard boxcars in freight trains, although several railroads equipped cars specially for this service.

Head-end cars include (starting behind the locomotive tender) express refrigerators, baggage express cars, and express boxcars. This westbound New York Central Detroit-to-Chicago mail and express train rolls through Niles, Mich., in April 1950. *Richard Pedler*

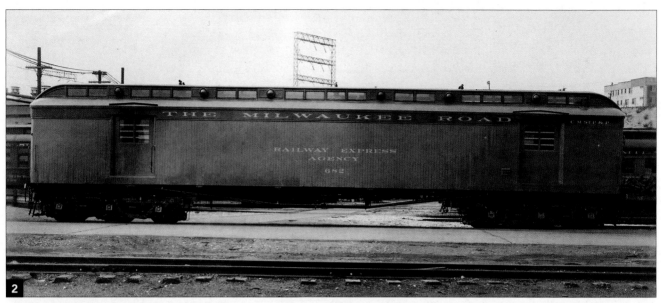

Baggage and other passenger cars were typically wood into the 1900s. This Milwaukee Road wood, truss-rod-underframe baggage car was built in 1907. *Milwaukee Road*

Seaboard Air Line no. 386 is a steel baggage express car with clerestory roof, four-wheel trucks, and twin (double and single) door openings. The star below the lettering indicates that it is equipped as a messenger car. *Bob's Photo*

Baggage express cars

The term *baggage car* is a bit of a misnomer because, although such cars were certainly used for passenger baggage, their primary use was to carry bags of U.S. mail and parcels for Railway Express Agency (REA). They are more accurately called baggage express cars, and the Association of American Railroads (AAR) classified them BE (see the table on page 39).

Baggage car design varied widely by railroad, as most were built to plans following other passenger equipment. In general, baggage cars have end doors, two sets of sliding doors on each side, and no windows.

Wood construction for passenger cars was typical until just after the turn of the 20th century but was far from ideal, **2**. In crashes, especially at high speeds, wood cars tended to disintegrate. They would also burn easily if a fire broke out. After 1900, some cars were built with steel underframes and a wood superstructure (which would become common for freight cars), but this could still result in telescoping or "riding over" in an accident, where a steel car or frame

could slide up and over the steel frame of a wood car, shearing off the car body and causing damage and casualties.

The solution was the all-steel passenger car, which used steel underframes with a plate steel superstructure or body, **3**. The resulting cars were very strong, fared much better in accidents, and rode smoothly. They also weighed much more than a comparable wood car, earning them the moniker *heavyweight car*. A typical heavyweight baggage car weighed 70 to 75 tons, compared to 50–55 tons for later streamlined cars.

This Union Pacific 69-foot Harriman-style baggage express car was built in 1931. The round-roof car has six-wheel trucks.
Union Pacific

Steel cars were required for mail cars after 1911, and steel construction became the norm for all passenger cars by 1912, and no wood passenger cars were produced thereafter. Many wood cars remained in service for some time, however: 26,000 in 1925 (just under half of all cars in service), 5,000 in 1935, and 2,000 by 1940.

Heavyweight baggage cars were typically 60 to 70 feet long (usually shorter than other passenger cars), with some extending to 80 feet. Six-wheel trucks were typical on longer cars, with some shorter cars having four-wheel trucks. Most had two door openings on each side. Door openings (and door and window style) also varied: many cars had one wide door and one narrow door, with one or two sliding doors for each opening. Door location differed, with doors placed closer to the ends or to the middle.

Early passenger cars had clerestory roofs, which have a raised middle section down the length of the roof, usually with vent openings along the sides to allow air circulation. From the 1920s onward, more cars were built with arched roofs, with the roof

AAR head-end car classifications

BE   **Baggage Express:** Passenger train baggage car with side doors suitable for baggage and express

BEM **Baggage Express Messenger:** A BE car equipped with a desk, safe, lavatory, and lights for a riding messenger; marked with a 6"-diameter, five-pointed star beginning in 1948

BH   **Horse Car:** Express car equipped to carry livestock, with or without stalls

BM   **Milk Car:** Insulated, nonrefrigerated car for carrying milk in cans or bottles

BP   **Refrigerator Express:** Insulated car, with or without ventilation

BR   **Refrigerator Express:** Insulated car with ice bunkers

BS   **Refrigerator Express:** Insulated car with brine tanks generally used for shipping meat products

BX   **Box Express** Boxcar equipped for passenger train service with steam and signal lines

CA   **Combined Baggage-Passenger:** Car with two compartments, baggage and passenger (usually a coach or chair car)

CAD **Combined Baggage-Diner:** Car with two compartments, baggage and a passenger compartment equipped for food service

CO   **Combined Mail-Baggage-Passenger:** Three-compartment car

CS   **Combined Baggage-Smoking:** Two-compartment car, baggage and a lounge or bar or buffet

CSA **Combined Baggage-Dormitory-Kitchen:** Three compartments including crew sleeping quarters

CSB **Combined Baggage-Dormitory:** Two compartments with crew sleeping quarters

CSP **Combined Mail Storage** or **Baggage-Dormitory-Passenger:** Three compartments with the passenger area often a lounge or smoker

This Burlington Route baggage car includes "fish racks" (grated floor areas for drainage), a messenger's rack and fold-up desk (right), and water and toilet facilities (in the enclosure at right toward the rear). *Chicago, Burlington & Quincy*

The Burlington's *Fast Mail* used a baggage-rider car at the rear. It had facilities for a flagman inside (toilet and water), with marker-light brackets on the end and a small window on the side at the end. *Wallace W. Abbey*

curving downward at each end, **4**. This design was easier to build using steel (and less expensive to create) than the clerestory design. Roof vents and fixtures (style and location) are another spotting feature.

Other spotting features include the side sheathing/rivet pattern, side sill or lower side skirting (many older cars have fishbelly-style side sills or center sills that become deeper at the middle of the car), location of handrails and other details, and truck style. Also look for the number of windows, the window pattern, and the window size (on cars so equipped).

Because they rode at the front of passenger trains, baggage cars required passenger fittings, namely a steam line (passenger cars were heated by steam through the 1960s) and a communication signal line. These lines all required couplings between cars. The signal line was marked by a smaller air hose with glad hand, positioned under the larger train line (brake) hose on each end. The steam line was a pipe, with an angled fitting at each end below the coupler. This had to be manually connected and disconnected each time cars were coupled (unlike the air hoses, which would simply separate when pulled apart).

Internally, these cars were big, open spaces where baggage, crates, mail sacks, and parcels could be placed. As with other passenger cars, baggage cars have end doors that allow access from neighboring cars. Unlike other cars, access was limited to railroad employees (or postal clerks and express messengers)—passengers were not allowed. The steam line would be run up into the walls to provide warmth in cold weather.

Some cars had shelves or racks for storing small items, and many had "fish racks" (grating on the floor) to allow drainage for items that required ice to be placed on them during transit (such as milk and cream cans and cases of seafood), **5**.

Some baggage cars used by Railway Express Agency were accompanied by messengers. These express messenger cars had basic facilities for the messenger, including a desk, toilet, sink,

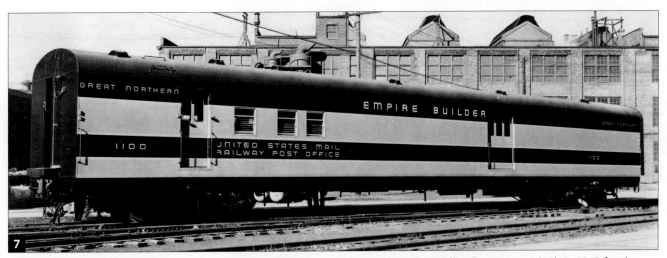

Baggage cars are sometimes combined with other cars. This is a 30-foot Railway Post Office/baggage car built in 1947 for the *Empire Builder*. *Great Northern*

drinking water, and lights. A safe was also anchored to the car and its steam line. Beginning in 1948, cars with messenger facilities were identified by a five-pointed star near the REA lettering. These were given AAR class BEM.

A variation on this was the rider car. On mail and express trains without a passenger car at the rear, space was needed for a flagman. Some railroads added a rider seat, toilet, water facilities, and marker-light brackets to baggage cars for this purpose, **6**.

Baggage cars were lettered for their owning railroads and painted in the owner's paint scheme (which could include a paint scheme for a specific train). Most cars also carried RAILWAY EXPRESS AGENCY lettering on the sides, and some had MAIL STORAGE or similar phrasing.

Combines, or combination cars, had two or more compartments, one of which was generally for baggage express. The other compartment could be a Railway Post Office (RPO) apartment and/or a passenger area (chair car or lounge), **7**. These were especially common on secondary and branch lines, where shorter trains didn't require as much space for baggage, express, and mail. Mixed trains often featured a combine instead of a caboose at the rear.

Some baggage cars were assigned to special duties. Notable were the cars assigned to the Atomic Energy Commission (Atlantic Coast Line 666

Louisville & Nashville no. 1652 is one of several baggage express and combine cars assigned to the Atomic Energy Commission. The L&N AEC cars were assigned to Oak Ridge, Tenn., and traveled with armed guards to other AEC facilities in the Midwest and West. *Both photos: Jim Seacrest*

This lightweight Rock Island baggage express car features fluted stainless steel construction, matching side doors, and four-wheel trucks. *Rock Island*

In the early 1960s, REA acquired several older baggage express cars. They received green paint and REA diamond logos. Many (like this one) were stenciled for rear-end service only. *Mainline Photos*

Express cars in service

Year	Baggage express cars	Total passenger cars
1915	9,900	63,000
1920	12,100	63,900
1925	13,200	65,600
1930	13,000	63,400
1935	10,300	50,500
1940	13,100	45,200
1945	13,700	47,200
1950	13,800	43,600
1955	11,100	36,900
1960	10,100	28,400

and Louisville & Nashville 1486 and 1652 were examples) to carry fissionable materials, **8**. These were lead-lined and no doubt contained other secret equipment. They were separated from other cars and always traveled with armed guards.

Car construction evolved significantly beginning in the mid-to late 1930s, as railroads began inaugurating new streamlined trains along many routes. These cars featured new construction techniques: some used fluted or corrugated stainless steel, **9**, while others had aluminum sheathing over steel frames or incorporated new lighter-weight steel alloys. The new methods saved a great deal of weight, and ushered in the term *lightweight car*.

For baggage cars, this meant the body styles followed the basic design of the rest of the train. Car sides were smooth or fluted, often with skirting extending below floor level. Gone were clerestory roofs and the rounded ends of earlier arched roofs, with the curved roof now extending all the way to the end. Many had full-width diaphragms on each end.

Lightweight cars allowed the use of four-wheel trucks, many with new designs. These new trains also ushered in new paint schemes. While most heavyweight baggage cars were dark Pullman Green with gold lettering, many new cars were painted in bright colors.

Comparatively few lightweight baggage cars were built. In most cases, a lightweight baggage car or two was built for each new train set but not enough to re-equip older passenger trains or to equip dedicated mail and express trains. Many heavyweight cars remained in service to the Amtrak era. Some kept their original schemes, while others were repainted to match streamlined cars and trains.

The change in REA's business model in 1961 led to the company acquiring ownership of many older baggage cars (as opposed to earlier, when railroads simply provided space for REA traffic in their baggage cars), **10**.

The REA-owned baggage cars were generally older heavyweight equipment, and they were painted green with REA EXPRESS lettering and one or two diamond logos on the sides. Many were used strictly as storage cars at the rear end of trains. These were stenciled with REAR END ONLY or similar lettering.

Express boxcars

Starting around 1940, many railroads began supplanting their fleets of baggage express cars with boxcars equipped for express and mail storage service. These were assigned AAR class BX, for box express, **11**.

Most were standard AAR-design boxcars but with high-speed trucks (steel wheels were also required for passenger service) to allow passenger-train speeds. Cars were fitted with steam and signal lines, so they could be carried at the head end of passenger trains, and often received high-speed (AB-1-B) brake systems. Many express cars received additional hardware, including a vertical grab iron to the left of the side door (in some cases, a short ladder), a stirrup step below the door, and a placard holder next to the door. Some also had marker-light brackets on one or both ends, so they could be carried at the rear of a train.

The largest fleet of express boxcars belonged to the Pennsylvania Railroad, which had more than 1,100 in service at one point. Most were versions of its common X-29 boxcars for both express and merchandise service. The express versions were Freight Car Red with RAILWAY EXPRESS AGENCY lettering, and as storage cars, they could be found in passenger trains of many railroads across the country, **12**.

Other major operators included Santa Fe, Union Pacific, Milwaukee Road, and Great Northern. As express traffic diminished from the 1950s into the 1960s, many of these cars were reconfigured for freight service, but some remained in express service until Amtrak.

Some railroads built cars specifically for express service, including UP, Milwaukee Road, and Santa Fe, **13**. The Union Pacific's 130 40-foot cars (class B-50-25 and B-50-31) were originally built for high-speed merchandise trains in 1939–1941, but were transferred

This Rock Island express boxcar has a steam line, signal line, EXPRESS lettering, a placard holder next to the door, and high-speed (roller-bearing) trucks. *William Raia*

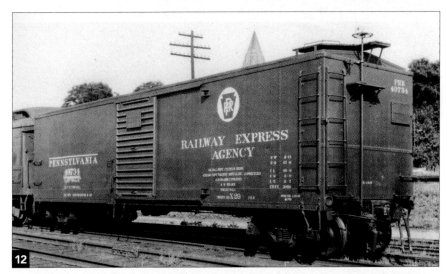

Pennsy had a large fleet of its X-29 boxcars equipped for express service, with REA lettering, under-door stirrup, vertical grab iron and placard next to the door, and steam and signal lines. *Pennsylvania Railroad*

Santa Fe had 350 50-foot express boxcars in three classes. Number 4182 is from the first batch, which was built in December 1941. It is riding on Allied Full-Cushion trucks. *Ted Culotta collection*

Union Pacific's express boxcars had a low profile (8'-6" interior height) and double doors, making them easy to spot. This car's original Elsey trucks have been replaced with A-3 trucks by the time of this late-1950s photo. *J. David Ingles collection*

Alton was one of several railroads to dabble with experimental aluminum boxcars for express service. Note the steam line (horizontal pipe) and signal line (small hose below the brake hose) for passenger service. *Alton*

Florida East Coast's ventilated express boxcars, built in 1945 by Magor (shown here in 1965), were equipped with Commonwealth high-speed trucks and steam and signal lines. *Robert A. Selle*

to express service by the early 1940s. Originally gray with CHALLENGER MERCHANDISE SERVICE lettering, they quickly received UP's yellow and gray passenger colors with EXPRESS SERVICE lettering, **14**.

Express service didn't require tall cars, so they were built with an 8'-6" interior height (two feet shorter than contemporary freight boxcars). They were built with high-speed trucks (Symington-Gould and others), had steam and signal lines, and featured double doors to speed loading and unloading. Their appearance and bright paint scheme made them easy to spot, and they often ran off-line and could be spotted in passenger trains on other railroads.

Most express boxcars were 40-foot cars, but the Santa Fe, Missouri-Kansas-Texas, and Missouri Pacific had 50-foot double-door versions and the Chicago & North Western, Chicago, Burlington & Quincy, Grand Trunk Western, and Southern had single-door 50-footers. Several other railroads had 50-foot cars rebuilt from former troop cars (more on those in a bit). The Pennsy had an oddball group of 10 60-foot cars with two separate door openings on each side. (You can see one in the background behind the locomotive in photo 10 on page 58.)

Lettering and paint schemes varied widely. Some were in railroads' standard freight schemes but with RAILWAY EXPRESS AGENCY, EXPRESS SERVICE, MAIL STORAGE, or similar lettering. Others were rather spartan, painted in black or Pullman Green with limited lettering (road name and express stenciling). Still others were painted in full passenger-scheme colors.

Some express cars carried full capacity and dimensional data like normal boxcars, which allowed them to be used in interchange freight service. Others had limited lettering (railroad name and number) like baggage cars, meaning they were limited to passenger train service.

Express cars often had lower load limits than comparable freight boxcars due to the high-speed trucks being used. The particular spring package used in the trucks limited the weight that could be carried but they improved riding characteristics. A star next to the load limit indicated that a car's load limit was less than a standard car of this type and that it could only be changed by the car owner.

The mid-1940s saw a flurry of experimental aluminum freight cars, usually built with the backing of one of the two major aluminum manufacturers (Alcoa and Reynolds). These followed contemporary AAR designs, with major components made of aluminum instead of sheet steel, **15**. Several became express cars, which was ideal because of the weight savings (about 2.5 tons lighter than a standard steel car).

Railroads with aluminum express cars included Alton (nos. 1200–1209), Great Northern (no. 2500), Nickel Plate Road (nos. 8500–8509), and Rock Island (nos. 20060–20069). They were distinctive and easy to spot because of their unpainted bodies, which went from a dull silver color when new to a dark, weathered gray as the cars aged.

A variation on the express boxcar is the express ventilated boxcar, **16**. Several Southeastern railroads, including the Atlantic Coast Line, Florida East Coast, and Seaboard Air Line, had fleets of ventilated express boxcars. These had slatted vents in the ends and/or sides, which, like refrigerator cars in ventilator service, allowed outside air to circulate through the car. This made them suitable for carrying produce as long as the outside temperatures were at or below the appropriate temperatures for that product. The vents could be closed, so the cars could be used in standard express service for conventional parcels.

Express reefers

As chapters 3 and 6 explain, many perishables (berries, first fruits of a season, plants, fruit gift baskets, and flowers) were shipped as express instead of standard freight. This and other LCL perishable traffic was handled aboard express refrigerator cars in passenger trains.

Express reefers were owned by Railway Express Agency as well as

This 50-foot Pacific Fruit Express wood express reefer has a radial roof and high-speed (Commonwealth) trucks. You can see the shadow of the fishbelly-style steel center sill in this 1951 view. *W.C. Whittaker*

Pullman-Standard built this steel 50-foot express reefer for Northern Refrigerator Car Co. in 1937. It has a straight center sill and Commonwealth trucks. *Pullman-Standard*

Built in 1929, Pennsylvania's 550 class R50b cars were among the first steel express reefers. They were 54 feet long, with a distinctive end roof slope and Pennsy 2D-P5 passenger trucks, and could be seen across the country. *Pennsylvania Railroad*

The Illinois Central converted 35 standard wood reefers to express service by adding high-speed trucks and steam and signal lines. *Mainline Photos*

Pacific Fruit Express no. 913 is one of 50 class R-40-10 steel cars converted to BR cars. The car was repainted olive green and given Chrysler FR-5 high-speed trucks and steam and signal lines. *Ted Culotta collection*

REA bought 500 new steel plug-door reefers from ACF in 1947 and 1948. They initially wore a green and aluminum scheme, but were repainted all green in the 1950s. *American Car & Foundry*

several railroads and private owners that also operated standard reefers, including Pacific Fruit Express, Northern Refrigerator Car Co., Burlington Refrigerator Express, and Western Fruit Express.

In the early 1900s, express refrigerator cars featured wood bodies and were typically 50 feet long (compared to 36 or 40 feet for standard reefers). Steel underframes gave many a distinctive look, with deep fishbelly side sills or underframes visible from the sides. Some wood express reefers had radial (rounded) roofs, **17**, while others

had peaked roofs. Roofs were typically canvas-covered wood. Trucks were passenger-style (Commonwealth were common), and these cars had a pair of swinging doors over a 4- or 5-foot-wide opening.

As with baggage cars, steel sheathing began replacing wood by the early 1930s, but the basic car designs remained similar to wood cars into the 1940s, **18** and **19**. Also, some wood express reefers were later rebuilt with steel sides. Major builders of these cars from the early 1900s through the 1940s included General American, American

Car & Foundry, Pullman, and various railroad shops.

Some express refrigerator cars were converted from standard reefers. An early example was the Illinois Central, which converted 35 wood-sheathed 42-foot cars built by AC&F in 1925 by adding high-speed equalized trucks and steam and signal lines, **20**.

The Pacific Fruit Express car in photo **21** is an example of a later standard car converted to express service. The REA needed additional cars to cover increased shipments in the early 1950s, and PFE modified

50 recently rebuilt R-40-10 cars with steam and signal lines, marker-light brackets, high-speed trucks, and high-speed brake systems. The cars were painted dark olive. They returned to freight service and were repainted orange in 1961.

The late 1940s and 1950s saw a round of new, "modern" express refrigerator cars. Railway Express Agency bought 500 new steel 55-foot ice-bunker cars from AC&F in 1947 and 1948, followed by another 1,000 cars from General American in 1955 and 1957, **22** and **23**. The cars were very similar in design, although the AC&F cars featured welded sides and the GA cars had riveted sides. The cars had sliding plug doors, GSC roller-bearing trucks, Preco air-circulating fans, steel roofs and running boards, and Dreadnaught ends.

Atlantic Coast Line bought 50 identical cars from AC&F at the same time as the REA order in late 1947 and early 1948, **24**. They were initially painted in the railroad's purple and silver scheme, but in the 1960s, they were repainted in a more subdued green scheme.

In 1952, the Great Northern bought new cars from Pacific Car & Foundry. The 50-foot steel cars had plug doors, fans, and GSC high-speed trucks. They were painted in GN's orange and green passenger scheme.

Express refrigerator car numbers dropped in the 1950s into the 1960s, following the general trend of refrigerator cars, as trucks had taken over most time-critical perishable shipments. By the 1960s, REA was the major owner of express reefers, but they spent most of their time carrying standard (nonrefrigerated) express parcels.

Paint and lettering on most express reefers was generally rather reserved. Pullman green or dark green were common, with the railroad name or owner on a letterboard along the top of each side. Additional lettering could include EXPRESS REFRIGERATOR or RAILWAY EXPRESS AGENCY, plus the car's reporting marks and number and, in some cases, the capacity.

General American built 1,000 riveted steel, plug-door express reefers for REA in 1957. They would spend more time carrying standard parcels than refrigerated shipments. *Railway Express Agency*

Atlantic Coast Line purchased 50 cars from ACF concurrent with the REA order in 1947–1948. They initially wore purple and silver. *Bob's Photo*

Express reefers—major owners

This roster includes the number of cars operated by all owners with at least 100 cars in any of the years covered. The total for each year includes all owners, not just those listed.

Owner	1933	1940	1947	1955	1961
Canadian National	245	227	240	324	376
Canadian Pacific	250	250	247	343	243
Great Northern	227	227	189	82	0
Illinois Central	526	118	79	20	0
Missouri Pacific	295	217	27	0	0
Northern Pacific	368	45	5	3	0
Northern Refrigerator	568	659	649	509	163
Pacific Fruit Express	298	298	289	188	136
Pennsylvania	586	585	582	415	130
Railway Express Agency	0	421	778	1,709	2,465
St. Louis-San Francisco	147	147	68	8	0
Union Refrigerator Transit	285	285	168	29	60
Western Fruit Express	387	100	99	79	31
Total in service	4,668	4,134	3,966	4,121	3,721

In the early 1950s, REA added large versions of its diamond logo to its cars, including express reefers such as this wood 50-foot car. *Mainline Photos*

Converted troop cars can be identified by their rivet patterns, marking the locations where the side windows were plated over. The Burlington had 300 of them. *Hol Wagner*

The REA broke from this design with its 1947 cars, which were delivered in a green-and-aluminum scheme with red striping and black and gold lettering. These cars were repainted a solid green during the early 1950s.

Also in the early 1950s, the REA added a large (60") version of its red-and-white diamond logo to its cars, **25**. The early 1960s saw the lettering change to REA Express and the car color became a brighter (apple) green, and the logo was also simplified.

Specific rosters, including detailed owner-by-owner rosters from the 1930s through the 1960s can be found in *Railway Prototype Cyclopedia, Vol. 7.*

Converted troop cars
Notable among fleets of express boxcars and reefers are cars converted from former World War II troop sleepers and kitchen cars. In 1943, the U.S. government ordered 2,400 troop sleeper cars (from Pullman) and 440 troop kitchen cars (from American Car & Foundry) to cope with the tremendous surge in passenger traffic during the war. At least 1,000 of these cars were later converted to express cars by several railroads.

These cars were based on then-current AAR designs for 50-foot boxcars. They rode on Allied Full-Cushion high-speed trucks and had reinforced ends with end doors, steam lines, and signal lines. After the war, the cars were considered surplus. Many railroads purchased

Troop cars converted to express reefers lost their end doors and received swinging plug side doors. The former window locations are readily visible. *Jim Seacrest collection*

them at bargain-basement prices and converted them to many uses. They were ideal for express service, since they already had high-speed trucks and signal and steam lines.

Express conversion usually entailed plating over the side windows (leaving a distinctive side pattern even after repainting), stripping the interior fixtures, and sometimes reconfiguring the side doors, and/or removing the end doors, **26**. Cars converted to refrigerator service had insulation added, new interior walls, new end ice bunkers, and roof hatches. The end doors were removed, and new swinging side doors added, **27**. Many kept their Allied trucks until the trucks were banned from interchange service in 1955. After that, cars were re-equipped with a variety of high-speed trucks.

Major owners of these rebuilds included Baltimore & Ohio, Chicago, Burlington & Quincy, New York Central, and New Haven. (The chart at right shows all owners.)

Converted troop cars in express service

Owner	Baggage	Reefer
Alaska RR	75	
Algoma Central	5	
Baltimore & Ohio	114*	
Boston & Maine	25	
Chesapeake & Ohio	18	
Chicago & Eastern Illinois	19	
Chicago, Burlington & Quincy	300	
Chicago, Rock Island & Pacific	50	
Delaware, Lackawanna & Western	11	
Fort Worth & Denver	2**	
Kansas City Southern		25
Minneapolis & St. Louis	3	
Monon	10	
New York Central	400	
New York, New Haven & Hartford	150	
Northern Alberta	2	
Ontario Northland	3	
Pacific Great Eastern	9	
Railway Express Agency	100	275
St. Louis-San Francisco	14	

* Includes 14 former C&O cars
** Former CB&Q cars

New York Central's *Pacemaker* cars were among the best-known merchandise cars. Note the limited data markings and how the vermillion has weathered on the car at right. *J. David Ingles collection*

Southern Pacific's distinctive B-50-15 cars were rebuilt for *Overnight* service from older wood-sheathed cars with new steel sheathing. Note the ladder and stirrup at the door. *Mainline Photos*

Merchandise cars

From the late 1930s into the 1950s, a few railroads began operating merchandise and LCL traffic in dedicated trains, many with specially equipped cars. Although slower than passenger trains, these LCL trains moved at speeds faster than standard freight trains and rated special attention.

Railroads took differing approaches to the cars used for merchandise traffic. Most simply used standard boxcars, but many equipped, painted, and lettered fleets of cars to handle the traffic, supplanting the special cars with general-service cars as needed. In some cases, these were older cars that were rebuilt, while others used new cars.

Among the most famous were the New York Central's distinctive vermillion and gray cars used for *Pacemaker* service, which was inaugurated in 1946, **28**. The railroad eventually assigned 1,000 cars to the service. The bodies were contemporary AAR 40-foot cars, but with a 10'-0" inside height, 6" shorter than standard. Cars had both Youngstown and Superior doors.

The cars initially rode on Barber high-speed trucks, with spring packages that allowed only a 25-ton load (Note the LOAD LIMIT: 50000 stenciling), compared to 50 tons for a common boxcar. This allowed a better ride, and the weight limit generally wasn't a problem for LCL cars. Cars were also equipped with cushioned draft gear and high-speed (AB-1-B) brakes.

New steel cars for *Overnight* service arrived in 1946 from Mount Vernon. Note the simplified scheme without a spelled-out road name. *Ted Culotta collection*

Another 25 Pullman-Standard PS-1 cars arrived in 1954. These had cushion underframes and 8-foot door openings (earlier cars had 6-foot doors).

The initial paint scheme featured all-white lettering, with only the load limit and light weight positioned under the reporting marks. No capacity or dimensional data was included, as this was a requirement only for interchange service, and the cars were not intended to leave the NYC.

Paint scheme changes included a switch to black lettering on the gray areas around 1950 and a change to the heralds in 1955, giving them a black background. Dimensional data was eventually added to the cars.

By the late 1950s, LCL service was declining, and NYC was focusing on Flexi-Van service, so the *Pacemaker* cars returned to the general boxcar pool. The trucks were replaced, giving the cars a 50-ton capacity, and they were repainted in the NYC's standard Oxide Red paint scheme.

The silver *Overnight* scheme debuted in 1956. After *Overnight* service ended, cars tended to keep rolling in this scheme through the 1960s. *Ted Culotta collection*

Another distinctive scheme that has been captured by many model manufacturers is Southern Pacific's *Overnight* service cars. The SP began painting cars for this Los Angeles-San Francisco LCL service black, with an *Overnight* logo in red with a yellow arrow. The class B-50-15/16 cars,

originally single-sheathed wood cars, were rebuilt with steel sheathing, giving them a distinctive appearance, **29**. A batch of new 450 B-50-24 boxcars arrived in 1946 for *Overnight* service. These were AAR 1944-design cars built by Mount Vernon but with a 10'-0" inside height, simplified lettering (the

Along with 40-foot cars, the Pennsylvania had 100 60-foot class X40B boxcars with 7-foot doors for merchandise service.
Pennsylvania Railroad

The Missouri Pacific rebuilt more than 1,000 older boxcars for its *Eagle* Merchandise Service. The stenciling at upper left states that the cars are to stay on-line and not be interchanged. *Missouri Pacific*

The Pennsylvania adopted a distinctive scheme for merchandise cars in the late 1940s (the service was named Keystone Merchandise Service in 1950). Cars had a wide horizontal gray stripe with thin white borders and MERCHANDISE SERVICE lettering, **32**. The bulk of the Pennsy's cars for this were older X-29 40-foot cars. The Pennsy also had 100 60-foot X40B boxcars with single 7-foot sliding doors and collapsible interior load retainers.

The Missouri Pacific in 1950 rebuilt 1,350 older boxcars for its *Eagle* Merchandise Service, **33**. The cars, 36- and 40-foot wood cars built in the 1920s, received new steel roofs and sides and a bold paint scheme. The sides had horizontal blue and gray bands (matching the *Eagle* passenger train colors), gray ends (blue by the late 1950s), and yellow doors. As with other railroads' special cars, these were designed to stay on-line (or on Texas & Pacific or other MP subsidiaries), but by 1960, they were repainted and in general service.

Other railroads painting cars for merchandise service included Baltimore & Ohio, the original Norfolk Southern, and Western Pacific.

spelled-out road name was eliminated), and distinctive additional vertical rivet lines on each side panel, **30**.

In 1956 this scheme changed to aluminum, to match the SP's piggyback trailer scheme, **31**. The arrow

logo disappeared and was replaced with simple OVERNIGHTS lettering in red under large SOUTHERN PACIFIC lettering. Cars wore this scheme until 1961, when *Overnight* service was discontinued.

1

CHAPTER FIVE

Depots, freight houses, and transfer terminals

Handling millions of carloads of express and less-than-carload (LCL) shipments required a significant investment in facilities, ranging from small-town depots and freight stations to large-city transfer stations and terminals, **1**. Let's first examine how these facilities were designed and handled this traffic, and then take a look at day-to-day operations at each.

Freight terminals coordinated merchandise boxcar movements, as well as those of trucks, for pickup and delivery. This is at the New York Central's freight station at Bellefontaine, Ohio, in 1949. *New York Central*

Combination depots

Most small- to medium-size towns along a railroad rated a combination depot, **2**. As the name implies, this means the station served both passengers and freight. There were close to 60,000 combination depots in service in the mid-1940s. In the days before radio, they were vital to railroads in terms of train operation, and they were primary originating and destination points for passengers and freight.

A typical layout featured a waiting room or two for passengers. Larger stations often had separate men's and women's waiting rooms, and depots in the South had segregated rooms. It also included an office for the agent and operator (and sometimes a separate express room or office) and a freight room. Located at one end of the building, the freight room had large doors on both the track and non-track sides of the building.

Most depots were built to standard plans established by each railroad, **3**. Each railroad's design featured common construction features and styles, including siding type, window and door styles, roof style, trim, paint schemes, and signs. The size varied based on the size of the town and the amount of passenger and freight traffic being handled—or what was expected—when it was built.

Many small stations would have a single operator-agent. The operator dealt with train orders, telegraphs and other messages, and railroad operation issues, while the agent dealt with local shippers and customers, rates and tariffs, handling freight, and passenger tickets. Larger stations would have a separate operator and agent, possibly a separate clerk or clerks and cashier, and separate Railway Express Agency (REA) employees. These positions varied by the amount of traffic being handled.

Most small to medium-size communities had a combination station. The Southern Pacific depot at Santa Ana, Calif., has a LCL boxcar parked next to the elevated platform on its house track in the early 1950s. *Tom Gildersleeve*

Located on a Milwaukee Road branch, Sisseton, S.D., had a small combination station. Note the Railway Express sign and the boxcar (no doubt of LCL) tucked on the house track behind the depot at right in this 1939 view. *John Vachon, Library of Congress*

Through the 1930s and 1940s, even small towns could generate significant LCL and express traffic. During that time, retail businesses often received cases of products in this way. It wasn't unusual for towns of 5,000 to 10,000 to have multiple REA delivery trucks assigned to the depot, with a local trucking company contracted to handle railroad LCL business. This traffic eventually went away as wholesalers and jobbers began supplying remote areas more and more with ever-expanding truck routes.

At local depots, originating LCL freight would come in, by a customer's own truck, by a local trucker contracted by the railroad (drayage company), or a railroad's own truck (more typically, a subsidiary trucking company controlled by the railroad). The freight would be weighed on the depot scale. Rates were based on 100-pound increments with a 100-pound minimum. Items were labeled and a waybill prepared for each shipment.

As chapter 3 explained, the depot and freight house would usually share space with the Railway Express Agency. Railroads in many locations contracted with REA to provide local pickup and delivery, and positions sometimes overlapped with work done at the depot.

Freight and express came in many forms and container types. This included cardboard boxes and cartons, almost any size of wooden crates, wood or metal barrels, steel drums, and cloth sacks and bags. Some items were bundled, such as wool, cotton, lumber, and pipe. Other items might be uncrated, such as steel castings or some types of machinery and machine parts.

Although forklifts, tractors, and other powered handling equipment came to many large freight houses and terminals by the 1940s, such luxuries were rare at local depots. Most small depots had to rely on old-fashioned hand trucks and tools (and creativity) through the end of LCL service in the 1960s.

Workers use a hand truck to unload LCL items from a peddler car (or waycar) on the Rutland at Florence, Vt., in 1958. *Jim Shaughnessy*

Baggage carts of mail and express have been positioned on the platform as Louisville & Nashville train 52 slows to a stop at Ashley, Ill., in September 1957. *Jim Shaughnessy*

A Railway Express Agency truck (right), along with a cart with milk cans, transfers express into a messenger car, while in the background, mail bags are loaded and unloaded from an RPO car along the Monon in 1948. *Linn Westcott*

Willmar, Minn., was a division point on the Great Northern, and it rated a separate freight house, shown here in 1939. Note the crane at the far end of the platform. *John Vachon, Library of Congress*

The hand truck was the standard method of handling most items that couldn't be carried by hand, **4**. Hand trucks could be pushed for moving small items or pulled in a low position for moving large, heavy items. Agents and laborers became adept at balancing and handling heavy loads that otherwise would have been impossible to carry by hand. Workers also used other four-wheel dollies and carts for heavier items, along with a variety of pipes, pry bars, crowbars, and poles as levers to lift and move heavy items.

Larger combination depots, especially at locations that warranted their own boxcars spotted to deliver and pick up LCL, were served by a "house track," a track that passed usually behind and along the depot. These would commonly pass beside an open parking area, allowing it to serve as a local team track as well. The station platform along the house track might be elevated to car-floor level, which allowed easier handling of freight in and out of cars, **2**. This was common for stations receiving and shipping a lot of LCL traffic. Other depots had a ground-level platform, so items had to be lifted to and from the car.

A house track could be a spur, but they were often double-ended to make it easier for trains from either direction to switch cars in and out of the track.

Many small-town and branchline depots had no house track. For these, the local freight would simply stop on the main line in front of the depot, unload and load freight from a waycar or peddler boxcar (more on those in chapter 6), and proceed on its way, **4**.

For loading and unloading express and mail, which arrived and departed aboard passenger-train baggage cars, the ubiquitous four-wheeled baggage

In 1916, the Illinois Central's Dubuque, Iowa, freight house had three tracks, including one that passed through the building. *Illinois Central*

The Illinois Central's Memphis, Tenn., freight house could hold more than 200 cars on its 10 tracks. It had separate inbound and outbound tracks and buildings divided by a platform between sets of tracks. *Illinois Central*

A Pennsylvania Railroad Geep pulls a string of express cars in front of Pennsy's Polk Street freight station. Polk was the country's largest freight terminal when built in 1918. *Ed DeRouin*

cart was the standard method, **5**. Carts were built to a number of designs, but all were similar, with a flat platform at car-floor height atop four wheels. A handle that raised and lowered the platform was connected to the front axle, which pivoted for turning. Carts were usually painted and stenciled with either RAILWAY EXPRESS or the owning railroad's lettering.

Carts would be loaded with outbound mail and express parcels in advance of a passenger train's arrival. The carts would then be pulled, usually by hand (some larger stations had powered tractors), and moved along the station platform as close to the position of the inbound cars as possible.

Loading could be for a single car for a branchline or a local train, but it could also involve multiple cars: REA parcels could go into one car, manned by a messenger, mail would go to the Railway Post Office (RPO), and passenger baggage in yet another car. Empty carts would also be positioned as needed to receive inbound shipments.

Trucks were often backed up directly to baggage cars, RPOs, and combines (as well as motor cars) to transfer express and mail, **6**.

Freight houses

A separate freight house was a step up from the combination depot. Freight houses were built in towns and small cities where traffic was heavy enough to overwhelm a simple freight room in a combo depot. Freight houses would generally receive and ship at least two or more cars a day, and 12 to 20 weren't unusual through the busy days of LCL service.

They were different from larger terminals or transfer houses as the primary purpose of a local freight house was receiving and shipping local freight and not transferring freight among several cars.

Locations varied. A freight house could be near or next to the passenger station or be several blocks away. As with combination depots, freight house design varied by railroad. Although most railroads followed a common construction design for depots and freight houses, adjusting the design for size, many were built unique to their location.

Small freight houses would be served by a spur or through track running alongside, with a loading dock at floor height, **7**. Larger freight houses might be served by two tracks, with

pass-through loading and unloading (in which cars are aligned side-by-side with bridge plates between doors) as with larger freight terminals, **8**.

A truck dock, either at the end or the non-track side of the building, would serve railroad-owned trucks for delivery and pickup, and local businesses could use their own trucks as well. Railway Express was likely to have its own facility adjacent to the passenger station for easier handling of express cars.

Transfer terminals

The biggest LCL-handling facilities were large-city freight houses (also called freight terminals, transfer houses, or transfer stations), **9**. What differentiates these from a small-city or local freight house is that their primary purpose is transferring LCL shipments among cars and sending them on their way to other large terminals. Delivery and pickup was also done from these stations, but the bulk of the traffic was just passing through.

The largest of these could handle several hundred cars at a time, with cars heading to and from other large freight houses both on-line and on other railroads across the country. Major junction cities, where multiple railroads met and terminated, were home to the largest facilities. Chicago, as the center of the country's rail operations and the primary connection point for many major eastern and western railroads, had the most freight houses (73 at one time), as well as the largest, and sent and received scheduled LCL cars to 40 states.

The largest of the early transfer stations was the Pennsylvania Railroad's Polk Street freight house in Chicago, which was built in 1918 as LCL traffic was growing, **10**. The building was five stories tall (with a 12-story clock tower in one corner), making it a prominent fixture in many photos taken near Chicago Union Station. The main (track) level and an underground tunnel system were used for LCL. The upper floors were used for warehousing, an integrated service operated by Western Warehousing Co., a Pennsy subsidiary.

The 450 x 745-foot building originally housed 19 tracks with room for spotting 375 boxcars. It also had 33 doors for trucks, along with docks for small shipments and perishables, and 32 freight elevators. It was notable for its modern freight handling methods in 1920, when it acquired a large fleet of electric tractors with cart trailers to haul freight between the storage area, docks, railcars, and trucks.

It typified the appearance of large-city transfer stations built in that period, with imposing brick

11

The Chicago & Eastern Illinois' Chicago freight terminal typified early big-city houses, with brick construction, multiple parallel tracks, and large surrounding city buildings. *Trains magazine collection*

construction that gave it a "city" look. Unlike small freight houses, transfer stations were generally built to a unique design to fit their surroundings. Many were constructed near passenger stations and rail yards in downtown areas, so they had to fit in with surrounding buildings, streets, rivers, and rail lines, **11**.

Polk Street was later superseded in size by the Chicago & North Western's massive freight house at Proviso Yard

in Chicago's western suburbs that was built in the late 1920s, **12**. This sprawling building started the trend for transfer stations being built away from city areas, where space is at a premium. The Proviso freight station was 500 x 900 feet and had 24 tracks, each holding about 36 cars, with a total capacity of 690 40-foot cars.

Specific design, size, and style varied among stations. Large painted signs on the walls often proclaimed the owning

LCL in refrigerator cars

LCL and mail were sometimes handled in conventional ice-bunker refrigerator cars, especially around Christmas and during other times of heavy traffic (see photo 23 on page 93). The Santa Fe and Union Pacific were the major users of reefers in this fashion. The reefers would be mainly loaded westbound, avoiding the usual empty movement for these cars, as most perishable traffic was eastbound.

Cars would be cleaned and deiced before being loaded with LCL. Permission would have to be obtained from the car owners for these movements (most commonly Santa Fe or Pacific Fruit Express), which usually wasn't a problem if they weren't needed right away for perishable loading—a paying return trip was better than an empty.

Clean, dry reefers were suitable as they were well sealed and protected their

contents well, but they were not liked by dock workers and agents. The doors were smaller: 4- and 5-foot-wide openings were common, compared to 6 feet for boxcars, making it harder to move carts and parcels in and out. Floor levels were higher, meaning bridge plates were angled, which made loading awkward, especially for heavy loads.

Cubic capacity was much less—because of insulation and end bunkers, ceiling

heights were lower, cars were narrower, and interior length was shorter (even with collapsible bulkheads) than boxcars. The typical formula was to swap two or three reefers in the place of one boxcar, which could make spotting at docks more difficult (especially at pass-through locations) and sometimes requiring them to be loaded at other locations, such as a nearby team track— further complicating and delaying the process.

Chicago & North Western's sprawling freight house at Proviso was located away from the city, taking advantage of the available space. *Jack Delano, Library of Congress*

Steel bridge plates allowed workers to load cars on parallel tracks. To do so, cars must be spotted precisely. *Pacific Electric*

railroad, with perhaps the railroad logo, city name, or specific station name.

To maximize the use of space, most had four or more parallel tracks adjacent to one side of the main building, relying on bridge plates placed between cars to allow workers to pass through one car to get to a car on an adjacent track, **13**.

Some terminals had a structure in a U shape (or simply parallel buildings) with four to eight stub-ended tracks inside the U. This allowed workers to load cars from both sides, with bridge plates only connecting half the cars. In this arrangement, one side was used for incoming loads and the other for outbound loads. Having separate buildings (or wings) for each simplified switching.

This loading arrangement was why 40-foot cars were preferred for LCL service, as spotting a 50-foot car meant that the adjacent spaces could not be used, as door openings wouldn't align for parallel cars.

The preferred design, where space allowed, was to have loading platforms between each pair of tracks, so the pattern was two tracks, loading platform, two tracks, loading platform, and so on, **14**. Advantages to this design

The New York Central terminal at Indianapolis had covered platforms between each pair of tracks. *New York Central*

were that bridge plates weren't required between parallel cars and that cars of differing lengths could be used, with cars not having to be uncoupled and precisely spotted to match parallel cars.

Loading tracks may or may not be covered, a design feature that varied depending upon the location and prevailing weather. The trend in northern climes was to have tracks inside buildings (as at Proviso), or at least have covered platforms between tracks, with platform eaves extending over the edges of cars.

Freight handling

Chapter 6 goes into detail on the extensive train and switching operations needed to serve large freight terminals, and it also explains how cars were assigned and routed. But first, understanding the many operations within the terminal will help you more realistically model freight terminals.

Once all inbound or outbound cars were spotted, each string of cars would be "blue flagged"—a blue sign or tag

was added to the end car to signify that workers were in, under, or on cars, **15**. This meant that a railroad crew could not couple to the cars until the flags were removed, which could only be done by the workers on the cars.

Boxcar doors were opened on the dock side, and both doors would be opened on any cars that required a pass through to get to a car on a parallel track. For cars along the dock and between parallel cars, bridge plates (steel plates of various designs) were needed to allow movement of hand trucks and other equipment. At large stations, most plates would be set in place by forklift, **16**. Some, however, relied on hand power, as a pair of workers would "walk" the plate into position (lifting and setting down alternate corners) and then lower it into place.

It took hundreds of workers within each terminal or transfer house to ensure smooth operations. The specific job names and duties of the dock and car workers varied among railroads and stations, but the basic job processes

were the same. The traditional method, called the *gang system* was to organize dock workers into crews of three to five. Each crew, or gang, was responsible for multiple cars, working them one by one.

A *checker* or *receiving clerk* was the head of the crew. He worked on the dock and was responsible for tracking each item going to or from a car. He kept a binder or clipboard of all waybills for each of the cars assigned to him, and matched all shipments against their waybills to ensure that all cars assigned to him had the proper items, **17**. (Unlike a standard freight car that used a single waybill for a carload shipment, an LCL car had an envelope that held all the waybills for one car, **18**.)

Each checker would be in charge of one or more *truckers, truckmen,* or *pickers*. These workers used hand trucks, carts, or power lift trucks to carry parcels to and from their assigned cars under direction of the checker.

Each crew had a *packer, loader,* or *caller* who would work in the cars,

The blue signs (flags) at the end of the cars signify that men are working on or in them, so they cannot be switched. This is Illinois Central's Water Street freight house in 1943. *Jack Delano, Library of Congress*

A forklift driver places a steel bridge plate between the dock and boxcar at Pacific Electric's Los Angeles freight house. *Pacific Electric*

having the responsibility of getting everything on and off the car or cars assigned to him, calling to the checker as the truckers carried parcels from the car, **19**. Items could be carried directly to another car or to an area in the freight house assigned to an outbound car.

The gang system was labor intensive, and its efficiency was limited in part by the number of workers who could simultaneously work among the docks and cars without getting in each other's way.

Loading technology changed in the 1920s and 1930s, as electric- and gas-powered tractors with trailers (carts) emerged, followed by forklifts and skid loaders, **20** and **21**. Automatic cart tracks became imbedded in platforms, and other advancements included intercom/speaker systems, pneumatic tubes for waybills and paperwork, and two-way radios.

As the largest stations began using these devices, they shifted from the gang system to the *drop-truck* system

by the 1930s and 1940s. In this system, a driver and helper would use a tractor to pull a long cut of trailers (four-wheeled carts), **22**. Starting in the freight house, carts would be loaded by stevedores, each item checked by a clerk, with merchandise on each cart headed for a specific boxcar. The driver/helper would then head to the dock and drop the trailers off at cars as needed. Stevedores or loaders would then load the boxcars.

The process reversed itself for inbound loads, with empty trailers dropped off at the boxcar locations and then picked up when cars were unloaded onto the trailers. Forklifts would be ready to handle loads that couldn't be picked up by hand. As with the gang system, a clerk checked each item against its waybill. The drop-truck system made huge installations like Proviso practical, and eventually led to automated cart systems at modern terminals.

Tractors and carts represented a significant investment, and their viability depended upon the installation's size and the length of hauls needed. Many medium to small stations kept using a form of the gang system with hand carts until the demise of LCL.

The man in charge of the whole operation was the station or terminal agent, who supervised a legion of

The checker or clerk makes sure that all items loaded and unloaded by the pickers or truckmen match the waybills. Note the uncrated gears on the hand truck. *New York Central*

assistants and clerks. The agent had final responsibility for ensuring that all cars were sealed and ready to be switched at their scheduled times. He and his assistants made sure all inbound and outbound shipments matched their waybills, reconciled any missing items (or items with missing waybills), dealt with damaged goods, and solved any other problems that arose.

Other personnel included a *cooper*, who fixed railcars as needed (especially car interiors) and repaired damaged crates and boxes, a *sealer*, who was responsible for opening and closing cars and applying seals to car doors, and a host of office and administrative workers. As you can imagine, in the days before computers, the amount of paperwork needed to process thousands of individual shipments was massive.

Along with boxcars, there was plenty of truck traffic at large terminals, so most had extensive docks for both trailers and smaller trucks, **23**. By the mid- to late 1920s, much of the local

LCL exchanged among freight houses in the same city was accomplished with trucks. It was easier and faster to use trucks for these short hauls— using boxcars typically added a day to shipping times.

Trucks would also be loaded for delivery to local customers, and inbound trucks (railroad owned, contracted, or those of customers) would drop off shipments as well.

Boxcar loading

Cars were generally loaded below their cubic and weight capacity. Scheduled cars operated regardless of the freight level that particular day, much like a passenger train will run regardless of whether there are 5 or 70 people boarding it. If that meant that a car started or ended its journey with only a few parcels in it, so be it.

The wide variety of material being handled could make it a challenge to load cars. Damage claims were a major expense for LCL because of the

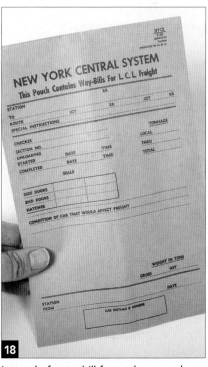

Instead of a waybill for each car, each LCL car had an envelope that held all the waybills for that car. *Jeff Wilson collection*

19

The packer, or loader, worked on the boxcar, directing the truckmen and checking each parcel as it was loaded or unloaded. *New York Central*

20

Forklifts came into wide use at large terminals by the 1940s. Crates like this were used in LCL cars to protect small parcels. *New York Central*

sheer number of items being handled, the disparate (and awkward) sizes of individual items, and the number of times shipments would be unloaded and reloaded. Railroads spent a lot of time and effort training their employees to handle items with care to prevent claims.

That started with the boxcars themselves. As chapter 4 explains, many railroads assigned specific cars to LCL service. Many received special paint schemes, but more importantly, they had been upgraded with equipment such as smooth-riding high-speed trucks, cushioned draft gear, and upgraded interiors.

Common boxcars also frequently carried LCL, but not just any car could be used. The easily damaged nature of merchandise traffic made it especially important that a car have an interior that could be well sealed, have a roof with no leaks, and have doors that sealed tightly. A single roof leak during a thunderstorm could result in dozens of separate damage claims.

Car interiors needed to be clean, with no stray nail heads, broken boards, or other protrusions that could damage lading or tear boxes or crates. Boxcars were graded by condition, from A through D and unrated, with A being the best. For LCL, railroads used A or B cars.

Cars would be loaded as evenly as possible to improve riding characteristics. Many items required special handling, and the American Association of Railroads (AAR) issued publications with illustrations showing how various items should be handled and secured. Plate glass, for example, was shipped in crates that had to stand on end (and some of these were large—imagine the front window of a store—and weighed hundreds or thousands of pounds). These would be positioned along one side and tacked into place to keep from shifting.

Uncrated items, such as machinery, castings, and pipe, could be blocked and tacked in place to the floor or side to keep it in place. If these heavy items shifted in transit, they could be damaged and also damage surrounding shipments—imagine a 500-pound steel gear casting breaking loose and crushing six cases of corn flakes.

Large, sturdy wooden crates and barrels would be placed on the floor, with lighter cardboard boxes and packages placed on top. Boxes would be packed in as tightly as possible to minimize shifting that could occur during operation. Many railroads used large open-top, wood-frame crates to hold small parcels that might be crushed by larger loads, **20**.

Pallets were used quite a bit around large freight terminals by the 1940s but generally just within the terminal. Unlike today, when loads are secured to pallets and transported with their loads, at that time, pallets were only used for in-house transfer, with the contents restacked in cars or trucks.

Once cars were loaded, temporary bulkheads or gates would be placed across the loads in each end, **24**. These looked like large pallets, made from wood with three or four vertical posts and several cross members, and were designed to fit the width of a boxcar. They allowed loads to be firmly secured regardless of how fully the car was loaded. Bulkheads would be positioned securely, with wood blocks nailed in place to hold them to the floor and each wall. In photos of freight terminals, you'll sometimes see stacks of bulkheads along platforms or next to buildings.

REA and mail

Railway Express and post office facilities operated in much the same fashion. They were separate from LCL transfer houses. The main distinctions were that REA was a single operating body, so there was no distinction between on- and off-line shipments or cars and that shipments traveled in baggage cars, express boxcars, and express reefers instead of standard boxcars.

Large-city express terminals and post offices were almost always adjacent to passenger stations, **25**. Their size and exact layout and design varied depending upon the amount of traffic handled and the layout of the passenger station, but they would have multiple tracks and loading docks for baggage and express cars.

Skid loaders and pallet jacks were also commonly used at large freight houses. *New York Central*

The drop-truck system, with powered tractors and cart trailers, replaced the gang system at many large terminals from the 1930s onward. This is at Seaboard Air Line's Hamlet, N.C., terminal in the 1950s. *Seaboard Air Line*

Trucks handled pickup and delivery as well as some inter-terminal traffic. A forklift unloads crated machinery from a Santa Fe trailer at Kansas City in the 1940s. *Santa Fe*

24

Temporary bulkheads were tacked and blocked in place to keep loads from shifting. Note the chalk marks for train numbers and destinations by the door. *New York Central*

They often had pairs of tracks with platforms in between to allow direct dock access, but many were also built with a pass-through design. This was not as common as in LCL terminals because of the size differences among baggage cars, as well as the varied door sizes and placements of individual cars.

REA terminals often had significant cold storage areas to handle perishable shipments. This varied by location—the Jacksonville, Fla., terminal, for example, originated many perishable loads, and thus was sufficiently equipped for this traffic, **26**.

Depending upon the size of the facility and train scheduling, inbound cars would be switched out of trains and spotted at the REA terminal. For other trains, baggage carts were used as at smaller stations. Carts would be placed along the station platform, with parcels loaded and unloaded once the train arrived at the station. The larger the station, the more likely that

Boston & Albany (New York Central) freight houses

Railway Express Agency

Boston South Station

Post Office

25

Railway Express Agency and post office terminals were often located adjacent to large stations, as here at Boston's South Station in the mid-1940s. *New York Central*

26

Railway Express Agency's Jacksonville, Fla., terminal handled many perishable shipments as well as standard express. This 1940s view shows several REA delivery trucks and trailers at the dock or the lot at right. *Trains magazine collection*

powered tractors would be used to move carts. Conveyors also came into wide use, **27**.

REA key-point terminals

In the early 1960s, REA opened dozens of what the company termed "key-point terminals" in both large and small cities throughout the country, **28**. As chapter 3 explained, these were designed to replace multiple smaller stations and agencies, with 20 to 40 delivery truck routes heading out of a single key-point terminal, instead of two or three trucks at dozens of smaller stations. Most had rail access, although tractor-trailers were being used more often for medium-length travel.

By 1964, REA had opened more than 50 of these terminals across the country. Some were in new buildings designed specifically for the purpose, while others were in older buildings that were leased or rented and reconfigured for the operation.

As the plan of the Nashville terminal shows, these terminals are very modelable (although the length would have to be scaled down a bit for most layouts), **28**. The Nashville

27

Modern REA terminals used a combination of powered conveyors and portable gravity rollers to sort parcels. *REA Express*

terminal had room for 6 rail baggage cars, baggage carts (wheeled in from the nearby passenger station), and 32 truck docks: 8 longer spaces for trailers and 24 shorter spaces for delivery trucks. The building also included a repair and maintenance garage for the local truck fleet.

Small parcels were handled using a combination of powered and unpowered (gravity) conveyor rollers

and belts. Inbound cars would be spotted, and a portable conveyor would be placed in a baggage car. Workers placed parcels on the conveyors, where they fed a larger conveyor. Depending upon the design, this would go to a central location, where the process was reversed and conveyors carried packages into outbound cars. Larger items would require separate handling with a fork truck.

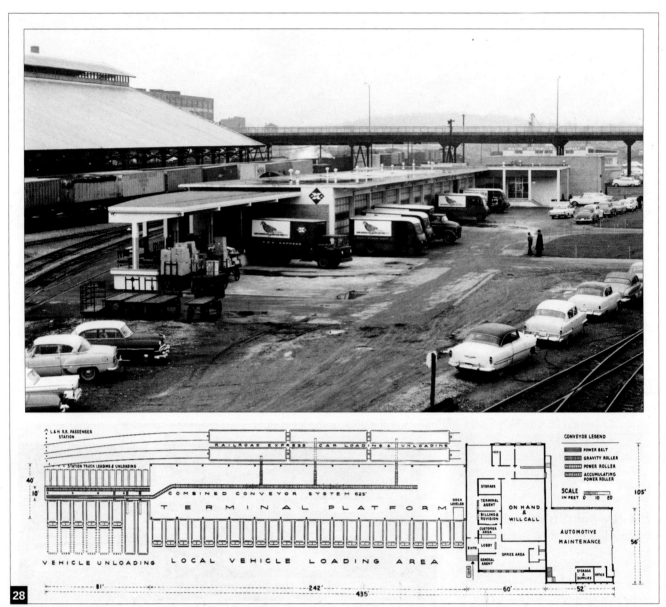

The diagram labels include:

L & N R.R. PASSENGER STATION

STATION TRUCK LOADING & UNLOADING

RAILROAD EXPRESS CAR LOADINGS & UNLOADINGS

COMBINED CONVEYOR SYSTEM 625'

TERMINAL PLATFORM

VEHICLE UNLOADING   LOCAL VEHICLE LOADING AREA

CONVEYOR LEGEND — POWER BELT / GRAVITY ROLLER / POWER ROLLER / ACCUMULATING POWER ROLLER

SCALE IN FEET 0 10 20

STORAGE / TERMINAL AGENT / BILLING & REVISION / CUSTOMER AREA / LOBBY / GENERAL AGENT / ENTR. / OFFICE AREA / ON HAND & WILL CALL / AUTOMOTIVE MAINTENANCE / STORAGE & SUPPLIES / OFFICE

DOCK LEVELER

40' 10' 105' 56'

81' 242' 435' 60' 52'

28

REA opened its Nashville key-point terminal in the early 1960s next to the Louisville & Nashville passenger station. *REA Express*

29

The Burlington opened a freight house near Chicago in 1958 with room for 184 cars and steel construction. *Burlington Route*

Modern terminals

In a last gasp to try to hold LCL traffic that hadn't been lost to trucks, several railroads that hadn't already left the merchandise business extensively rebuilt transfer stations or built new, large-scale freight stations and terminals in the mid- to late 1950s. These included:

• Great Northern's freight house at Gavin Yard in Minot, N.D. Built in 1956, the building was 102 x 600 feet with 4 through tracks holding 52 cars and with 200 platform trucks on a continuous conveyor chain.

• Chicago, Burlington & Quincy's Chicago freight house (officially Freight House No. 8 at Cicero Yard in Berwyn), **29**. Built in 1958, the building was 340,000 square feet, with 8 covered tracks and a capacity of 184 cars. It featured automatic conveyors and retractable bridges that could extend across the tracks.

• Santa Fe's Argentine (Kansas City), Kan., freight house, **30**. Built in 1961, the 330,000-square-foot building was 1,744 feet long, had 4 covered tracks holding 102 cars, had a continuous cart track, and provided docks for 231 truck trailers.

Construction of modern buildings usually featured prefabricated steel, with long, low structures that covered the tracks as well as the platforms themselves. Storage space was limited, with no warehousing and all loads being transferred among railcars and trucks. As with C&NW's earlier Proviso building, these new facilities were usually located away from cities (or at the fringes) where space was plentiful.

Most newer transfer houses featured continuous conveyor chains that guided carts in an endless loop around the platforms. With its Trukveyor system, Link-Belt was the biggest supplier of these. Two types were used: One had a slot in the platform over a chain. A peg on each cart placed in the slot would guide it at a constant speed around a loop. The second type used an overhead chain. Carts could be engaged and disengaged using a lever.

The automatic conveyors were an advancement of the drop-truck

Opened in 1961, Santa Fe's new Argentine freight house featured a continuous cart track around the platform. *Santa Fe*

system, requiring fewer workers to handle freight. The usual operating method would be to label carts with a destination (city or station name, train number, or boxcar number). The cart would then be taken off the chain at the appropriate boxcar.

By the mid-1950s and after, freight houses were sending and receiving fewer cars, and many were simply taken out of service. At many locations, railroads leased space in freight houses to freight forwarding companies—seemingly ironically, the companies that were taking the LCL business from the railroads, but in fact, these forwarders were often partially or wholly owned subsidiaries of the railroad. Railroads would still switch these cars of the forwarders, with the difference that they were now handled as carload freight instead of LCL.

By the late 1960s, the era of railroad LCL was all but dead. Many transfer terminals and freight houses were abandoned, torn down, or sold and repurposed. However, some continued in service for decades as warehouses, small manufacturers, feed stores, or other uses.

Modeling

How you model these facilities will largely depend upon the era you model and the specific railroad and locations

you model. For local depots, you can include a house track and platform for a car or two of LCL. Be sure to include an REA truck or two if you model any period into the 1960s, and have a few baggage carts on the platform ready to load and unload express from baggage cars as passenger trains make their stops.

Separate freight houses can be treated as an industry. Even a small one can rate three or four cars on a small or medium-size layout. Include railroad-owned or contracted trucks in the scene, ready to make local pickups and deliveries.

Large terminals can be modeled, and can be a focal point and/or major industry on a layout. You'll likely have to scale back the size using selective compression—perhaps include four tracks that each hold five cars, with the structure against a backdrop, or additional track space that passes behind the backdrop. You can have lots of carts, workers, and a variety of loads standing by, along with trucks, stacks of bulkheads, lift trucks, and other details.

These will require significant switching operations two to four times daily, with cuts of cars that will sometimes have to be separated and spotted individually to get door placements to match. Chapter 6 provides more detail on operations that can be modeled.

1

CHAPTER SIX

Train and car operations

Milwaukee Road's westbound *Morning Hiawatha*, train 5, pauses at Portage, Wis., in October 1965. Tucked behind the E units are several head-end cars, including a Great Northern express boxcar, Milwaukee express boxcar, and GN baggage express car. *Tom Hoffman*

Merchandise, mail, and express cars traveled across the country in a well-choreographed operation. These cars didn't travel randomly: they were scheduled as tightly as passenger trains, with schedules published and distributed to shippers and customers.

Peddler cars (or waycars) carried LCL to multiple stations along a route. Some were specially equipped and manned by messengers, as is this car on the Wabash at Marshfield, Ind., in 1948. *Ralph E. Byers*

Some railroads used side-door cabooses to carry LCL on branch lines. Here, the St. Louis-San Francisco crew has just unloaded several empty milk cans at Steelville, Mo., in 1949. *Frank Barry*

Express shipments, along with mail (more on that in chapter 7) traveled via passenger trains, while cars of less-than-carload (LCL) traffic were carried in freight trains, **1**. Let's first take a brief look at LCL car and train operations.

Chapters 2 and 5 explained how basic merchandise operation works. At a local depot or freight house, this could start by accepting anything from a single parcel or piece of crated machinery to 15 cases of paint. It could also be a distributor in a large city filling a car with hundreds of boxes bound for individual customers. These items were all combined and loaded onto cars for their destinations.

Car movements
They might all look the same from the outside, but boxcars loaded with LCL merchandise served several purposes. Many terms were used to describe cars in various types of service. Not all railroads used the same terms, and there was some crossover and duplication of words, but here is a general summary of the most common types of LCL cars:

Package or merchandise car: Can refer to any car carrying LCL shipments, but when these nonspecific terms are used, it usually refers to cars being handled on-line—among freight houses, transfer stations, or combination depots on the host railroad.

Ferry car: Ferry cars were loaded at a freight house or transfer station on one railroad and destined to carry, or *ferry*, parcels to a freight house on another railroad. Short-haul interline movements of ferry cars (such as between two freight houses in Chicago) were among the first LCL traffic that moved to trucks; longer ferry moves could be extensive—a thousand miles or more.

Overhead car (also called **through car**): This was a carload of LCL that a railroad picked up at an interchange, handled over a route, and turned over to another railroad at interchange, with no rehandling of the contents.

Peddler car (also called **waycar**): Peddler cars were used to distribute LCL to multiple stations along a route, **2**. They would be loaded at a larger freight house or transfer station. Peddler cars served stations too small to warrant receiving their own LCL cars.

At each station, parcels would be unloaded and loaded. Depending upon the railroad, a messenger may or may not ride in the car. Some railroads equipped cars especially for this purpose, usually with additional grab irons or ladders adjacent to the door. Other railroads used standard boxcars. Branches with light traffic might be served by a side-door caboose with a storage area, **3**. A local freight could carry more than one peddler car, depending upon traffic volume.

The local may simply pause at a station for the peddler car to be unloaded; if the train had other work to do in town, the local would set out the peddler car at the depot until it was ready to depart and then pick it up.

Peddler cars became less common after the 1930s, as many small depots were closed and railroad-owned trucks began serving many others.

Trap car: This was a car loaded with LCL items by a shipper on a rail siding at its own factory or warehouse. The shipper would load the entire car (or multiple cars), but the items were all individual shipments heading to multiple customers. The railroad would pick up this car and bring it to a nearby freight terminal, where it would be unloaded and the individual parcels sorted to their ultimate destinations.

Major users of trap cars included catalog companies, such as Sears and Montgomery Ward, that shipped out many cars of merchandise a day. Grocery and dry goods wholesalers and distributors also shipped products to their retailers this way.

Many short-haul (within-city) trap car movements gave way to railroad-owned (or contracted) trucks through the 1930s and 1940s, as they allowed faster service.

Line car: A variation of the trap car, the line car was similar, in as it was loaded by a single shipper with items for multiple customers.

Erie's 14th Street freight house in Chicago had seven tracks and was surrounded by rail yards. *Erie*

Several of Missouri Pacific's distinctive *Eagle* service merchandise cars are being switched at Broadway and Poplar Streets in St. Louis in the 1950s. The cars were restricted to on-line LCL service. *Missouri Pacific*

A Milwaukee Road switcher pulls a cut of cars near the freight house in Dubuque, Iowa, in the early 1960s. *Ed DeRouin*

However, instead of going to a freight house for unloading or reloading, the car was designated to stop at multiple consignees, usually along a single route.

Here's an example: An appliance distributor in a large city has five or six items for each of four retailers in small towns. The towns are 500 miles away, but all are located near each other on the same rail line. The car is delivered to the freight house or combination station in Town A and items for the first consignee—let's say three refrigerators and two stoves—are unloaded. The car is then picked up by the next local freight train and dropped off at the freight house in Town B, and the process is repeated.

Terminal operations

As chapter 5 explained, large freight stations and transfer terminals had multiple tracks, each holding several cars. A capacity of 60 to 100 cars was common; the largest stations could hold 200 or more cars.

Some terminals had combined inbound and outbound tracks, but the larger the station, the more likely that inbound and outbound tracks would be separate. This could mean separate docks, or buildings or docks

By the 1940s, railroads were using tractor-trailers to cover many LCL routes, especially on branch and secondary lines. This is the New York Central at Bellefontaine, Ohio, in 1949. *New York Central*

on either side of a central group of tracks, or completely separate buildings. Having these tracks separate simplified switching.

Transfer terminals were usually adjacent to major freight yards, so they were served by switching locomotives from the yard, **4**. Inbound LCL cars arriving in the yard were pulled from their trains, and cuts of these cars were then shoved into the inbound tracks at the transfer station. Specific times varied among freight stations, but cars were generally spotted overnight or in the early morning.

At terminals with parallel tracks, where workers passed through cars to work other cars, switch crews often had to uncouple cars and align them so that door openings matched on parallel tracks. The appearance of a 50-foot car or two could disrupt the car order.

At houses where bridge plates weren't used (where tracks were paired with with platforms separating them, so all cars were directly worked at a platform), switching was easier. Since all cars loaded directly to a dock, cars could be left coupled, and car length wasn't an issue (except for the total length of the track).

Once all inbound cars were spotted, they would be blue-flagged. The doors would be opened, bridge plates added, and terminal workers could begin unloading merchandise.

A switch crew would spot outbound cars (empties for loading) in similar fashion. Because outbound cars were assigned to a specific destination, either on- or off-line, these spotting assignments weren't random. They were based on future switching moves, so when the switcher pulled the loaded cars to a nearby yard, the cars were already blocked in proper order to save time in making up outbound trains.

For example, railroads that used specially equipped and painted cars for LCL generally kept them on-line. (As chapter 4 explained, the New York Central's initial *Pacemaker* cars were restricted from interchange because of their limited lettering; MoPac's *Eagle* Merchandise cars were likewise for on-line movements only.) So if these special cars were available, they would be the first choice for on-line destinations. If not enough special cars were available, the railroad's own standard boxcars would be the next choice (and high-grade boxcars would be preferred).

Likewise, per car interchange rules, for off-line moves, a car of the destination railroad would be the first preference. If an Illinois Central freight house was sending a car to the Monon, it would use a Monon car if one was available. If not, a foreign-road car in the direction of the

Monon would be the next preference, and so on.

This was an ideal situation. In practice, car-use rules weren't always followed to the letter, especially at terminals where inbound cars were immediately reloaded for outbound moves.

Cars were generally loaded during the day, with a cutoff time in the late afternoon (although there were exceptions). Following the cutoff time, bridge plates would be pulled, and the doors would be closed and sealed. The switch crew would be ready to start pulling cars as soon as the blue flags were removed. The switcher would pull all the tracks, taking the cars back to the yard, where the cars—blocked for their destinations—would be added to originating or through trains as required.

Problems and challenges could arise. If traffic was heavy to a destination, a second car might be required, taking up another spot. More cars arriving than expected could also present challenges—perhaps a delayed car or two arriving a day late, along with a few extra trap cars loaded by a busy local distributor. This could overwhelm the number of spots available at the terminal tracks. A car may have been held out or spotted at a nearby team track.

Now, let's take a look at how this worked.

A single-axle Pennsy trailer with the Keystone Merchandise Service logo on the front is positioned on a flatcar in Chicago in 1954. *Pennsylvania Railroad*

The Boston–Albany section of the *Pacemaker* pauses at Worcester to pick up cars in August 1949. *Philip Hastings*

Car routing

LCL cars had specific assignments and routing. These schedules were continually being updated based on traffic volume. Most railroads published these schedules in brochures or pamphlets. (Tracking one down can help tremendously in figuring out how all the operational pieces fit together. Check railroad historical society websites and publications, as many have published information for freight houses on their railroads.)

Not every freight house sent a car to every other freight house. Freight houses may have more inbound than outbound cars (or vice versa), depending upon local businesses, proximity to other railroads, and prevailing traffic patterns.

As an example, let's look at Missouri Pacific's Kansas City freight terminal in the mid-1950s. The summary of its daily inbound and outbound car movements from that period, shown on page 75, is a composite from multiple MP publications (including one on the Missouri Pacific Historical Society website, mopac.org).

In this period, the MoPac's KC terminal dispatched 50 LCL cars (most daily), including six waycars that cover multiple small stations along their routes. Included were

17 cars bound off-line for 13 other railroads.

Inbound traffic included 37 cars, including 20 from other railroads. At that time, the terminal also relied on truck routes for connections with another 8 on-line stations.

There wasn't always a match for inbound and outbound cars. For example, Kansas City received inbound cars from Cincinnati and New York City originating on the Baltimore & Ohio, but only dispatched a car to the B&O at Cincinnati.

Outbound cars at the terminal would be lined up in an order that would minimize later switching. Cars that were departing on the same route (or outbound train) would be placed next to each other. For example, the cars headed to the New York Central (East St. Louis and Indianapolis) would likely be placed together, along with the other East St. Louis car (for Louisville & Nashville).

Cars heading west on MoPac's line to Pueblo, Colo., would likewise be blocked together. This would include the Denver and Salt Lake City cars (both bound for Rio Grande), the San Francisco car (destined for Southern Pacific via Rio Grande), and the on-line cars for Pueblo and Hoisington, Kan.

The westbound on-line cars (Pueblo and Hoisington) would quite likely be

the MoPac's distinctive blue, gray, and yellow *Eagle* Merchandise Service cars, while the cars bound off-line would likely be Southern Pacific and Rio Grande (or other western-road) cars, **5**.

Small stations

Just as cars at large terminals were scheduled, so were cars at small freight stations and combination depots. A combination station at a large town or small city might receive its own car or two of LCL every day; a stand-alone freight house in a small city could receive a half dozen or more cars a day, **6**.

Continuing our MoPac example, let's look at a typical small-town station: Newport, Ark., at the time, a town of about 5,000 located about 85 miles northeast of Little Rock on the MP's main line to St. Louis. Newport had a combination depot, and as was typical for small to medium-size towns and cities, it received more LCL cars than it generated.

In the mid-1950s, Newport received three cars of LCL a day: one each from Little Rock, St. Louis, and Memphis. It loaded out just one: a car to Little Rock (where all merchandise would be unloaded and resorted). It was also served via truck from Batesville, Ark., and Hollister and Poplar Bluff, Mo.

Trucks

Most railroads owned or controlled subsidiary trucking companies to handle pickup and delivery of LCL, **7**. These trucks were often painted in the railroad's paint scheme, with large heralds, but the cab door featured the name of the trucking company. Examples included the MP's Missouri Pacific Freight Transport Co. and the Southwestern Transportation Co. of the Cotton Belt (St. Louis-Southwestern).

By the 1940s, as railroads cut back service on many branch and secondary lines, both cutting back the number of trains and closing many small depots, they found it more expeditious to handle LCL distribution by truck rather than by a peddler car on a local freight train. This was known as *substituted service*, and it could involve a straight truck or a tractor-trailer. These routes increased in scope and length through the 1950s.

As with LCL cars, these truck routes were scheduled movements. Going back to our MP example, there were eight substituted-service truck routes heading out of the railroad's Kansas City terminal in the mid-1950s. Many large railroads (including the Santa Fe and others) operated extensive truck lines for this service.

A lot of early trailer-on-flatcar (TOFC or *piggyback*) traffic was railroad LCL. Instead of loading and unloading railcars, trailers would be loaded, placed on a flatcar, and sent to their destination freight house.

By the 1950s, many railroads were operating LCL service with piggyback, including the Burlington, Baltimore & Ohio, Chicago & North Western, Great Northern, New Haven, Northern Pacific, Pennsylvania, Soo Line, Santa Fe, Southern Pacific, Union Pacific, Wabash, and many others, **8**.

Train scheduling

Into the 1930s, LCL cars—although themselves on specific routes and assignments—generally traveled in standard manifest freight trains, which included a mix of all types of freight cars, including cars of LCL, along with assorted other carload boxcars, tank cars, gondolas, and hoppers. Through

Missouri Pacific Kansas City LCL cars, mid-1950s

Outbound to	Railroad
Albuquerque*	AT&SF
Cincinnati*	B&O
Clearwater-Hardtner, Kan.**	
Coffeyville-Wagoner, Okla.**	
Concordia, Kan.	
Crane, Mo.	
Denver*	D&RGW
Durand, Kan.	
East St. Louis*	L&N
East St. Louis*	NYC
Eldorado, Kan.	
Falls City, Neb.	
Fort Scott, Kan.	
Fort Smith, Ark.	
Fort Worth, Texas*	T&P
Hoisington, Kan.	
Houston	
Hutchinson, Kan.	
Independence, Kan.	
Indianapolis*	NYC
Jefferson City, Mo.	
John Sevier Transfer* (Knoxville, Tenn.)	SOU
Joplin, Mo.	
Little Rock, Ark.	
Memphis	
Milton-Larned, Kan.**	
Muskogee, Okla.*	KO&G
Nehawka-Lincoln, Neb.**	
Nevada, Mo.	
North Platte, Neb.*	UP
Nowata, Okla.†	
Oakland, Calif.*	WP
Omaha	
Omaha*	C&NW
Pittsburg, Kan.	
Pittsburgh, Pa.*	PRR
Poplar Bluff, Mo.	
Potwin-McPherson, Kan.**	
Pueblo, Colo.	
St. Louis	
Salina, Kan.	
Salt Lake City*	D&RGW
San Antonio	
San Francisco*	SP
Sioux City, Iowa*	C&NW
Springfield, Mo.	
Topeka, Kan.	
Wichita	
Wichita*	AT&SF
Yuma, Kan.-Hastings, Neb.**	

Inbound from	Railroad
Atlanta*	SOU
Birmingham, Ala.*	L&N
Carthage, Mo.	
Chattanooga, Tenn.*	SOU
Chicago IC	
Chicago MILW	
Cincinnati*	B&O
Cleveland*	NKP
Cleveland*	NYC
Coffeyville, Kan.	
Columbus, Ohio*	PRR
Denver*	D&RGW
Durand, Kan.	
Fort Smith, Ark.	
Indianapolis*	NYC
Jefferson City, Mo.	
John Sevier Transfer* (Knoxville, Tenn.)	SOU
Kannapolis, N.C.*	SOU
LaGrange, Ga.*	A&WP
Lincoln, Neb.	
Little Rock, Ark.	
Louisville*	L&N
Louisville*	SOU
Memphis	
Nashville*	NC&StL
Nevada, Mo.	
New York City*	B&O
Omaha	
Omaha*	C&NW
Osawatomie, Kan.	
Pittsburgh, Pa.*	PRR
Pueblo, Colo.	
St. Louis	
Salina, Kan.	
Spencer Transfer, S.C.*	SOU
Springfield, Mo.*	SLSF
Wichita	
Osawatomie, Kan.	
St. Joseph, Mo.	
Sedalia, Mo.	

*Off-line movement
**Peddler cars, tri-weekly
†Tri-weekly

Truck service

Truck service was available in these cites:

Atchison, Kan.	Marshall, Mo.
Council Grove, Kan.	Osawatomie, Kan.
Joplin, Mo.	St. Joseph, Mo.
Leavenworth, Kan.	Sedalia, Mo.

The Missouri Pacific's Speedboxes allowed customers to pack groups of smaller parcels and send them as a single shipment. *Missouri Pacific*

Speedboxes came in multiple sizes. They could be wheeled on their own or carried by forklift. *Missouri Pacific*

freights and locals (or way freights) alike during that period were generally slow affairs.

From the 1930s onward, trucks began taking more and more LCL traffic away from trains. To combat this, railroads began focusing on reclaiming LCL with speed. The first all-LCL train, Cotton Belt's *Blue Streak*, started in 1931 (see photo 7 on page 17). Other lines implemented fast-freight service, combining merchandise as well as carloads of priority freight.

The *Blue Streak* was extremely radical for its time: a dedicated LCL train offering coordinated truck delivery tied to overnight service. It was especially notable because it took place during the Depression by a struggling railroad, the St. Louis Southwestern (Cotton Belt Route), and along a route that didn't sound like prime territory—East St. Louis to Pine Bluff, Ark., with connections into Louisiana and Texas.

The idea of running a dedicated merchandise train—and doing it at passenger-train speed—was radical. A switcher pulled cars from St. Louis at 6 p.m. for a 7:10 *Blue Streak* departure from Valley Junction (just across the Mississippi), arriving in Pine Bluff at 5:15 a.m. The train dropped off cars at intermediate towns where trucks were waiting to be loaded for morning deliveries. The first train on October 1 ran with 9 cars; by early 1932, 15 cars was common.

Other railroads followed the Cotton Belt's lead, albeit on routes between larger cities. These included the New York Central, with its Buffalo-New York City *Merchandiser* train in 1934 (which also carried perishable freight) and Southern Pacific, with its San Francisco-Los Angeles *Overnight* trains starting in 1935.

World War II interrupted many of these operations, as huge traffic increases called for railroads to move all freight (LCL as well as carload) as expeditiously as possible.

Post-war operations

As chapter 2 noted, the years immediately after World War II saw a small upturn in LCL traffic, and railroads created dedicated LCL services in an effort to keep the traffic from trucks. The *Blue Streak* continued, expanding its routes to Los Angeles as the *Blue Streak Merchandise* over Cotton Belt parent Southern Pacific. The SP also resumed *Overnight* service with specially painted black (later silver) cars (see chapter 4).

Among the most famous LCL services was launched in 1946, as the NYC specially equipped a fleet of 425 cars (eventually expanding to 1,000) and painted them vermillion and gray for its new *Pacemaker* LCL service, **9**. The all-LCL train initially ran between New York City and Buffalo, departing New York in the evening and arriving in Buffalo at 6:50 a.m., dropping off and picking up cars at Albany, Rochester, and other intermediate points.

Although *Pacemaker* trains weren't moving at *20th Century Limited* speeds, they were faster than standard freights, with a top allowed speed of 65 mph. Train length was capped at 75 cars, and 25 to 50 cars were common.

Service was added from Boston to Buffalo in 1949, and other routes soon followed, extending the service to Cleveland and Chicago. *Pacemaker* service was also offered on other parts of the system, including Indianapolis and St. Louis, albeit on standard fast freights where LCL cars were mixed with other cars.

The continued downward trend of LCL continued, however, and *Pacemaker* service was discontinued in the late 1950s. By 1960, most of the dedicated cars had been repainted into standard NYC colors.

The NYC's chief competitor, the Pennsylvania, also worked hard to retain merchandise traffic. The Pennsy launched its own dedicated LCL service in 1947, officially calling it Keystone Merchandise Service beginning in January 1950. The Pennsy labeled specially equipped cars with a horizontal aluminum (later white) stripe with MERCHANDISE SERVICE lettering. Most were the railroad's older X-29 40-foot cars, rebuilt with load restraining devices, but the railroad had 110 60-foot cars as well. The fleet reached around 700 cars by the mid-1950s.

Express/mail train consists
Union Pacific train 6 (the *Mail and Express*, Ogden-Council Bluffs), 1950

Car type	Origin/Destination	Received from	Delivered to
Express	Los Angeles-Chicago	No. 38 at Ogden	C&NW No. 6 at Omaha
Express	Sacramento-Chicago	SP No. 22 at Ogden	C&NW No. 6 at Omaha
Express	Oakland-Chicago	SP No. 22 at Ogden	C&NW No. 6 at Omaha
Storage Mail	Sacramento-Council Bluffs	SP No. 22 at Ogden	—
Storage Mail	Oakland-Chicago	SP No. 22 at Ogden	CB&Q No. 8 at Council Bluffs
Storage Mail	Ogden-Council Bluffs	—	—
Storage Mail	Los Angeles-Council Bluffs	No. 38 at Ogden	—
RPO	Ogden-Council Bluffs	—	—
RPO	Ogden-Denver	—	No. 52 at Cheyenne
RPO	Cheyenne-Omaha	—	—
Storage Mail (2)	Portland-Council Bluffs	No. 18 at Green River	—
Storage Mail	Oakland-Council Bluffs	SP No. 22 at Ogden	—
Storage Mail	Oakland-Chicago	SP No. 22 at Ogden	CB&Q No. 8 at Council Bluffs
Storage Mail	Oakland-New York City	SP No. 22 at Ogden	CB&Q No. 8 at Council Bluffs
Storage Mail	Oakland-Chicago	SP No. 22 at Ogden	CB&Q No. 8 at Council Bluffs
Coach	Ogden-Council Bluffs	—	—

Union Pacific train 17 (the *Portland Rose*, Denver-Portland), 1950

Car type	Origin/Destination	Received from	Delivered to
Mail-Express	Denver-Green River	—	—
Storage Mail (2)	Council Bluffs-Portland	No. 5 at Green River	—
RPO	Green River-Portland	—	—
Bag-Express	Chicago-Portland	No. 5 at Green River	—
Bag-Express	Salt Lake-Pocatello	No. 24 at Green River	—
Mail-Bag-Exp	Salt Lake-Portland	No. 33 at Pocatello	—
Mail-Bag-Exp	Kansas City-Portland	No. 369 at Denver	—
Coach	Chicago-Portland	No. 23 at Green River	—
Coach	Kansas City-Portland	No. 37 at Denver	—
Coach	Denver-Spokane	—	—
Diner	Denver-Pendleton	—	—
Club Lounge	Denver-Portland	—	—
Sleeper	Denver-Portland	—	—
Sleeper	Kansas City-Portland	No. 37 at Denver	—
Sleeper	Chicago-Portland	No. 23 at Green River	—
Sleeper	Salt Lake-Spokane	No. 33 at Pocatello	—

Source: Union Pacific Historical Society *Streamliner*, Vol. 4, No. 3

The Pennsylvania ran its trains on several routes, including New York–Chicago, New York–St. Louis, and Chicago–St. Louis. Its symbol freight trains had LCL prefixes, and these trains handled both LCL cars as well as freight forwarder traffic.

Although both the New York Central and Pennsylvania had fairly large fleets of cars specially painted and equipped for LCL service, many standard boxcars were also used for merchandise.

In 1950, the Baltimore & Ohio introduced Timesaver service for LCL freight (and a matching service, called Sentinel, for carload shipments). Service was available system-wide, initially with dedicated trains operating from New York to Philadelphia, Baltimore and St. Louis.

Another dedicated service with special equipment was Missouri Pacific's *Eagle* Merchandise Service in 1951. The MoPac rebuilt a fleet of older boxcars for the service and

Northern Pacific's westbound *Mainstreeter* carries several head-end cars as it rolls near Missoula, Mont., in 1966, including four NP express baggage cars, a Union Pacific baggage car, and an RPO. *Philip C. Johnson*

Seaboard Air Line motor car 2027 leads local train 11 near Rochelle, Ga., in 1947. The RPO apartment is part of the motor, and the REA express messenger gets some air in the open door of his car. *D. W. Salter*

painted them in distinctive blue, gray, and yellow. The MP started with 490 cars, and had almost 1,400 cars by 1953.

Most *Eagle* service was handled in conventional fast freights, but the MP did operate a dedicated LCL train from St. Louis to North Little Rock.

An innovation for the MoPac was the use of Speedboxes—miniature containers that could hold small lots of LCL cases and parcels for individual consignees, **10**. The boxes came in various sizes from 42 to 74 cubic feet and could hold up to 1,200 pounds. They had wheels and could be rolled on their own or handled by a cart or

forklift, and they could be easily loaded aboard a boxcar or truck, **11**. By 1953, the railroad had 651 Speedboxes in service.

Eagle service lasted through the 1950s, but declining revenues caused the operation to move entirely to trucks by 1960, spelling the end for the specially painted cars.

These named services with special cars received a lot of attention from the railroad press (and also railfan photographers), but they were the exception rather than the rule. Most railroads simply handled LCL in standard freight cars in scheduled priority freight trains.

Express head-end operations

Express parcels (Railway Express Agency traffic) and mail traveled in passenger trains, usually in baggage cars (more appropriately baggage express cars) but sometimes in express boxcars and express refrigerator cars. (Chapter 4 goes into detail on the equipment involved.) This is known as *head-end traffic*, as the cars were carried at the front of trains, ahead of passenger cars, **12**.

Through the 1940s and into the 1950s, passenger trains still traversed most routes across the country. Many locations still saw multiple trains in each direction every day. All trains did

The second section of Santa Fe train 20, an eastbound express mail train, descends Edelstein Hill by Chillicothe, Ill., around 1950. Six express reefers trail the locomotive, followed by several baggage express cars. *T. H. Cole Jr.*

not perform all functions, either with passengers or express shipments.

At the top of the list were front-line name trains, the flagship long-haul trains for each railroad. Famous examples include the New York–Chicago *20th Century Limited* of the New York Central and *Broadway Limited* of Pennsylvania, Northern Pacific's *North Coast Limited*, and Santa Fe's Chicago–Los Angeles *Super Chief*. These trains featured the fastest schedules and the most luxurious equipment, catering to first-class travelers. Although most carried a Railway Post Office car, few handled significant head-end traffic.

The next tier included secondary trains. Some were regional, such as the Chicago & North Western's *Capitol 400* between Chicago and Madison, Wis. Others duplicated long routes of luxury trains, but operated on slower schedules, with more stops and more emphasis on coach travel, such as the Northern Pacific's *Mainstreeter*. These trains often carried significant numbers of head-end cars—in many cases, more head-end cars than passenger cars—and often a manned (messenger) express car.

Following that were the local trains. These were unnamed, numbered trains

A New Orleans Union Passenger Terminal switcher gets ready to add a Southern Pacific express boxcar (with Allied trucks) to a passenger train in 1954. *James G. LaVake*

(although sometimes given nicknames) that generally served all stops on a given route, with coach service only, **13**. They generally operated between key junction or division points, as well as on many branch lines. Some, especially on branch lines, were covered by gas-electric motor cars. They typically included an RPO car, and could have a messenger car as well.

In their own category were mail and express trains, **14**. These were first-class trains, but generally wouldn't appear in public timetables. They were made

up of solid baggage and express cars (often 20 or more cars), but either had no rider cars or perhaps a single rider coach at the rear.

Most were unnamed, but many carried the unofficial moniker of *Fast Mail* or *Mail and Express*. They were responsible for carrying a great deal of the scheduled intercity storage mail and express cars in the country. (Chapter 7 includes several examples of their operations.)

The chart on page 77 lists the consists of a pair of Union Pacific

The engines from Burlington *Fast Mail* train 29 prepare to couple to a baggage express car after setting out a car. The steam line made it more time consuming to switch head-end equipment. *Wallace W. Abbey*

trains, circa 1950, to illustrate how this traffic was handled. One, the *Portland Rose*, was a secondary train operating between Denver and Portland. It was left to handle most head-end traffic along that route, as the flagship train, the *City of Portland*, didn't carry head-end cars.

The other train, No. 6 (unofficially the *Mail and Express*), was an Ogden, Utah, to Council Bluffs (Omaha), Neb., train that—in spite of its lone rider coach—was essentially an all mail express train that connected with similar trains of the Southern Pacific at Ogden and the Chicago & North Western and Burlington Route at Council Bluffs/Omaha.

Along with scheduled cars, trains could carry additional head-end cars, such as extra mail and express cars (especially during the Christmas rush), cars intended for other trains that missed their connections, or express reefers for seasonal shipments.

When head-end traffic became especially heavy, additional trains were added to the schedule. For ease in dispatching, these would usually be run as a second section of an existing passenger or express train. For example,

the start of the strawberry harvest in California in April might mean a few solid trains of express reefers moving from California to Chicago and then to New York. Because the refrigerator cars all required multiple re-icings en route, it was easier to handle them as their own train, separating them from other head-end cars.

Switching operations

As with LCL cars, outbound express and mail cars would have specific cutoff times at their originating terminals so they could be sealed and switched to their appropriate trains. A terminal switcher would spot the outbound passenger train consist at its platform at a prescribed time before departure (this could be as much as two or three hours for evening trains with sleeping cars, allowing passengers to board at their leisure).

Passenger cars (sleepers, coaches, diner, and lounge) were placed first. The head-end cars would be added later, as close to departure time as possible to allow a longer cutoff time, **15**. Cars from connecting trains would be added upon their arrival, again by a terminal switcher. The road power would be added last.

Head-end cars were blocked whenever possible to make future switching moves (en route setouts and end-of-run transfers) easier. Certain cars may also have to be in specific positions relative to Railway Post Office cars for access to storage mail.

At intermediate terminals that mainly served through trains (trains that didn't originate or terminate at that station), any sealed outbound through cars would be sealed in time for a train's arrival. The inbound train would be separated, and if a switcher was on duty, it would pull express and/or mail cars on and off as needed (otherwise the passenger train's road power would make the move), and the train was reassembled and sent on its way. This was a longer process than with a freight train, as the steam line had to be disconnected and reconnected along with the brake and signal lines, **16**.

If no cars were being switched, any mail and express shipments would be waiting on carts on the platform by the train's arrival. Items would be loaded and unloaded to the RPO, a mail storage car, or an express messenger car in the train in similar fashion to operations at small stations. More than one train could serve the same town multiple times during a day.

The best way to accurately model these operations is to follow schedules, train lists, and photos for the railroad, era, and location you're modeling. The book *Moving Mail and Express by Rail* by Ed DeRouin goes into detail on these operations and provides train consists and other detailed information for several railroads. Railroad historical societies are another excellent source of information. Many have published train consists and summaries of operations in their official publications, and some have this information on their websites.

As chapters 3 and 7 explain, the amount of express and mail carried began dropping significantly from the late 1950s into the 1960s, tied to the drop in number of scheduled passenger trains. By 1970, most express and mail traffic had disappeared from railroads.

Canadian express and LCL companies

The story of U.S. LCL service is told in chapter 2 and Railway Express Agency is covered in detail in chapter 3, but express and LCL operations were significant north of the border as well. Canada's two major express companies were, unsurprisingly, tied closely to the country's two largest railroads, Canadian National and Canadian Pacific.

In 1921 the Canadian National Express Co., which traced its roots to 1854, consolidated with the Canadian Express Co., operating over the Canadian National and its affiliated lines. At the time of the merger, the company had 3,500 offices and served 24,000 miles of railroad.

In 1882, the Canadian Pacific acquired the Dominion Express Co., which had been founded in Winnipeg in 1873. In 1926, the railroad renamed the company Canadian Pacific Express and moved its headquarters from Winnipeg to Toronto. By the following year, the company had 7,000 offices and served 31,000 railroad miles.

As with REA in the United States, the Canadian companies handled all manner of shipments, from parcels to valuables to livestock and refrigerated shipments. Express was handled in passenger trains, many using messengers as with REA. Also as with REA and LCL traffic in the states, Canadian parcel traffic dropped off from the 1940s through the 1960s. Canadian express companies had to submit rates to the Board of Railway Commissioners and have them approved by the governmental group.

Both companies evolved by establishing trucking lines to handle both express and LCL and offering air express services. In the late 1940s, CP established Canadian Pacific Transport as a piggybacking subsidiary, and in 1960, the railroad established CP Merchandise Services to handle LCL (including trucking). These also operated with several other CP subsidiary trucking companies throughout Canada. The largest was Smith Transport, of which CP gained full ownership in 1962.

In the 1970s, Smith and other subsidiaries were combined with CP Merchandise Services and CP Express to form CP Express and Transport. The merger wasn't enough to save the LCL and express business, and the division struggled. Employees bought out the company in 1994 and renamed it Interlink Freight Systems, but it ceased operations in 1997.

Canadian National formed the Canadian Express Cartage Department to provide trucking services in the late 1930s; the LCL division and express division operated separately. Delivery and pickup for LCL was in red-orange trucks featuring the CN shield and TRANSPORTATION LTD. or CARTAGE SERVICES lettering; after 1953, the lettering became FREIGHT. Express trucks were painted blue with gold lettering and a rectangular "wafer" herald (changed to the maple leaf herald after 1953) and CANADIAN NATIONAL EXPRESS (later just EXPRESS) under the herald. The services faded by the 1960s, and were largely gone by the 1980s, replaced by standard piggyback services.

A Canadian National express agent makes a delivery in the mid-1940s. *Canadian National*

A baggageman loads express and LCL aboard a combine on a mixed train on the Canadian Pacific (Quebec Central) at Vallee Junction, Quebec in May 1959. *Jim Shaughnessy*

Canadian Pacific Express and Canadian National Express both experimented with containers that could be moved from flatcars to truck chassis. *Canadian Pacific*

1

CHAPTER SEVEN

Moving mail by rail

Picking up mail on the fly was a signature service along Railway Post Office routes. Here, the catcher arm on an RPO car has just snagged a pouch of mail from the mail crane along the New York Central. *A. C. Kalmbach*

For more than 100 years, mail was the highest-priority commodity carried by U.S. railroads. Railroads competed for lucrative mail contracts along their routes, and the passenger trains that carried storage mail received preferential scheduling and treatment. Not only did railroads carry mail, but clerks sorted and prepped mail while trains were in motion, picking up and dropping off mail, often while trains were moving, **1**.

The first true Railway Post Office cars, where clerks sorted mail en route, were built for service on the Hannibal & St. Joseph in 1862. *Burlington Route*

Clerks sort mail on the St. Paul & Aberdeen RPO on Milwaukee Road train 15 in the spring of 1968. *Don L. Hofsommer*

AAR mail car classifications

MA	**Postal Car:** Railway Post Office (RPO) car for sorting mail in transit. Cars are lettered UNITED STATES MAIL RAILWAY POST OFFICE
MB	**Mail-Baggage:** Two compartments, RPO and baggage
MBD	**Mail-Baggage-Dormitory**
MBE	**Mail-Baggage-Express:** Three compartments
MD	**Mail-Dormitory**
MP	**Postal Car:** For transporting newspapers and large packages
MR	**Postal Storage:** For carrying mail in bulk, with no sorting equipment
MS	**Mail-Smoker:** Combination RPO and smoker/lounge car

The first mail moved by train in 1831, and the Baltimore & Ohio established a regular route (Baltimore to Frederick, Md.) in 1832. It was a natural move, as railroads were expanding and provided fast, reliable routes and service compared to riders on horseback or horse-powered stages. The government recognized this, and a congressional order made every railroad a postal route as of 1838.

At first, railroad cars simply carried mail. The next step was to have someone ride along with the mail to handle it at stations, making exchanges and accepting letters. This began in 1840 on lines from the Boston area to Norwich, Conn., and Springfield, Mass.

The birth of the modern Railway Post Office (RPO) was in July 1862. William A. Davis, a former postmaster at St. Joseph, Mo., was frustrated with mail trains on the Hannibal & St. Joseph (a Burlington predecessor) running late because of the time it took to sort mail at stationary offices before loading it aboard the train.

Davis had the idea that mail could be sorted while a train was in transit. His idea was adopted, and a converted baggage car was placed in service on the route across Missouri, **2**. The experimental car only ran a month or so until specially constructed cars entered service in August of that year.

That service, which lasted about a year, was designed to get mail to a stage line at St. Joseph (and delivered the first mail to the Pony Express). Credit for the first permanent RPO car and route goes to the Chicago & North Western from Chicago to Clinton, Iowa, in 1864. That service differed from the original in that intermediate towns along the route were also served, and mail was sorted for destinations beyond Clinton.

The Railway Mail Service was created in 1869 as the branch of the Post Office responsible for mail by rail. In 1875, the first all-mail train—and the first of many to be dubbed the *Fast Mail*—began running from New York to Chicago on New York Central System lines.

Railway postal clerks were federal employees. Here, a clerk works on the last RPO in service, New York & Washington (on Amtrak), in October 1972. *Don L. Hofsommer*

Mail bags are transferred from a Milwaukee Road RPO on the eastbound *Midwest Hiawatha* at Davis Junction, Ill., in the early 1950s. Trains *magazine collection*

Service grew dramatically as railroads expanded routes throughout the country. In 1875, mail service covered 70,083 route-miles. By 1900, the service had more than doubled, to 179,982 miles, with 1,300 RPO routes serving the country.

Railroads provided service to virtually every town on their routes (and many that were off-line as well). Large cities generated multiple cars of mail. Smaller cities were served by passenger trains that paused to load and offload multiple bags of mail. Small towns were served by moving trains that picked up and dropped off individual mail pouches on the fly.

Brick-and-mortar post offices sorted mail and served as the base for mail carrier routes, but railroads were responsible for handling more than 90 percent of intercity mail for at least part of its journey well into the mid-1900s, **3**.

By the mid-1920s, railroads hosted 1,500 RPO routes, with 10,000 trains carrying mail along more than 230,000 miles of railroad. As with express, LCL, and other rail traffic, the Depression diminished the number of trains and routes, as well as the overall volume of mail, but that traffic picked up again during and immediately after World War II.

In 1944, railroads handled 22.2 billion pieces of mail, carrying 93 percent of mail for at least part of its journey. This was highly profitable for railroads, which that year received $128.3 million in payments for handling mail. The top earners were the Pennsylvania at $14.7 million and Santa Fe at $10.2 million. By 1953, total payments would be $310 million.

However, as earlier chapters discussed, after the war, Americans abandoned passenger trains in droves, moving to automobiles and improved highways as well as airlines. Since passenger trains and mail were dependent upon each other, it created a domino effect: If a passenger route was discontinued because it was losing money, that was one fewer route and connection for mail; if a mail contract was pulled, the passenger train handling it likely went away because it could no longer be profitable. As more trains disappeared, so did their connections, which slowed and limited mail schedules.

The Post Office began routing more mail by airplanes and trucks in the 1950s. A lot of remaining mail started moving "closed pouch" only, moving from post office to post office without being sorted en route in an RPO car.

The Railway Mail Service officially became the Postal Transportation Service in 1949. Eliminating the word *Railway* in the title foretold the future, even though railroads still hauled a significant amount of mail in the 1950s. In 1956, railroads handled 56 billion pieces of mail—a record—and still served 39,000 locations, but a growing portion of it was storage mail, as RPO runs had dropped to around 600.

Mail contracts and routes continued dropping, from 262 RPO routes in 1961 to 190 by 1966. Along with diminishing passenger train routes, other factors included the emergence of large mechanical sorting and canceling machines in the 1950s, with the Post

Office decision to sort mail in large regional centers, followed by the move to ZIP codes in 1963.

The biggest downsizing came in 1967, when most rail mail contracts were canceled. When railroads turned over passenger operations to Amtrak in 1971, seven of the eight remaining RPO routes were canceled. The last RPOs, on New York City–Washington, D.C. trains 3 and 4, made their last runs in June 1977.

Basic mail handling

The country was divided into 15 divisions, with published Railway Post Office routes for each division, which covered almost all rail routes in the country that had passenger service. RPO routes were numbered, and were listed with their train numbers. RPO routes were known by the end points of their routes (the first city is the northern- or easternmost on the route), such as Chicago & Omaha or Duluth & St. Paul, and which appeared on their cancellation stamps.

First-class mail was sorted ("worked") aboard the RPO cars, while lower-class mail was carried in mail storage cars but added to mail being delivered on a route. The mail was carried in several types of canvas bags. The term *bags* includes pouches, which were used for first-class mail, and sacks, for non-first-class mail. Pouches and sacks each came in three sizes.

The mail was handled by railway postal clerks, who were federal (not railroad) employees, **4.** Clerks were initially hired after passing civil service tests, and had to pass regular, stringent examinations that demonstrated their ability to handle mail. Each clerk had to know every town in their three- to five-state division, along with the route each town was on and the order of the towns. Clerks also had to know how a letter would be routed for the next leg of its journey beyond his train, so they had to know all connecting RPO routes, along with those routes' end points and connection points.

Clerks (at least those assigned to handle registered mail) carried sidearms. Through the 1800s, train robberies were not uncommon; mail

Highway Post Office

This Highway Post Office bus, shown in 1948, was operated by Gulf Transport, a subsidiary of Gulf, Mobile & Ohio. *William Lavendar*

The Highway Post Office (HPO) was a service begun in 1941 in response to declining rail passenger routes, with an ultimate goal of replacing the RPO system. Each HPO was a bus, outfitted with an interior like a RPO car with cases, pouch racks, and sorting tables. Clerks worked mail in transit, stopping to pick up and drop off mail at post offices along the route. Outside, the buses wore various red, white, and blue paint schemes with HIGHWAY POST OFFICE lettering.

The first route started in February 1941 between Washington, D.C. and Harrisonburg, Va. World War II slowed HPO's growth, but additional routes were added beginning in 1946. HPO routes were generally short, around 150 miles, because of limited onboard storage space and the need to refuel buses.

By 1954, there were 134 HPO routes: 10 were operated by railroads, 65 were run by the Post Office itself, and 59 by private contractors. HPO routes grew into the early 1960s, but then began declining, doomed by the Post Office's sectional centers and their mechanical sorting machines. The last route, Cleveland & Cincinnati, was discontinued in 1974.

and express cars were usually the targets, as a lot of registered mail included payroll cash, cash traveling among Federal Reserve Banks, and other valuables.

RPO cars were built to one of three standard layouts, with a working interior area ("apartment") 60, 30, or 15 feet long. The walls were set up with an arrangement of slots or pigeonholes for sorting mail. Each set of pigeonholes was called a "case," with the number of cases varying by the length of the car. Cars also included pouch racks, which held bags for sorting.

The number of clerks working on each car varied. A branch line or secondary route using a 15-foot apartment might have a single clerk and possibly a helper. A 30-foot

apartment might have 3 to 5 clerks, while a full RPO car could have 6 to 10 clerks. Major trains might carry more than one working RPO car depending upon the volume of mail.

Positions were divided, with a chief clerk, second clerk, and third clerk, down to casemen and pouch helpers. Each had specific duties regarding sorting mail, handling registered mail, and preparing pouches for picking up and dropping off mail on the fly.

Mail was sorted aboard the car to various levels depending upon its final destination. The idea was that each letter is initially sorted to a pouch for a region, then state, particular railroad, specific route, and then town or post office.

For example, if a clerk on an RPO in Georgia doing an initial sort of

Where mail volume was high, the mail messenger would park his truck on the platform to transfer bags. *Ted Shrady*

The combined eastbound *Super Chief/El Capitan* approaches the mail crane at Los Cerrillos, N.M., on the Santa Fe in January 1962. *Clinton W. Morgan Jr.*

Great Northern mail clerk Ben Russell grabs the pouch from the catcher after making the catch at Bethel, Minn., while working the Duluth & St. Paul RPO in fall 1968. *Don Hofsommer*

mail picked up at a small town sees an address of Montana, he wouldn't be concerned with a specific RPO route. It would go into a slot (and then a pouch) labeled for that state. At the next transfer point, the pouch would go into a storage car headed north to Chicago and then Minneapolis. As it headed west it would be pulled out of storage, along with Montana-bound letters from other regions of the country, and sorted into slots for specific routes and towns.

However, if that clerk's next letter had an Atlanta address, he would not only put it into a slot for that city, he would likely have a slot for a specific local post office or even a carrier route.

A clerk's job began before departure time—sometimes several hours earlier. The RPO car would be on the ready track with the rest of the train. When clerks arrived, they would "dress the racks"—prep the car by labeling all of the slots in their cases and setting the pouch racks. They then began sorting mail before the train's departure.

Stamps were postmarked at their originating location, so clerks would postmark any letters that were "dropped" at the car or at mailboxes at station platforms. Clerks had bags of mail to sort from the originating station and then sorted any mail picked up at intermediate locations. Failing to complete sorting by the end of a run resulted in demerits; if a clerk received too many, he could lose his job.

Mail was picked up and dropped off at stations along the route. Larger towns and cities might warrant a full mail storage car to be dropped off and picked up. More common were towns with multiple mail sacks to transfer, but not enough to make up a full car. For these, a train would stop and mail would be transferred in and out of the RPO or a working storage car. This could be two or three sacks at a small town, or enough sacks to fill the rear of a truck in a small city.

A local mail clerk or mail messenger (someone contracted by the post office) would bring mail sacks to the depot in advance of the train. Baggage carts might be used, **5**, or the messenger could simply drive his vehicle (station wagon, pickup truck, or full-size truck) onto the platform for the transfer, **6**.

However, the most distinctive method of mail transfer was reserved for small towns.

Mail on the fly

A distinctive feature of RPO operations was picking up mail "on the fly," using a hook on the side of the RPO car to make a "catch" by snagging a mail bag from a lineside stand, **1**. The practice began in the 1860s, and was initially done by hand from the moving train—a dangerous task. The crane/catcher design was developed quickly, and it was safer and allowed higher speeds for the exchange.

The process was used at thousands of stations across the country, mainly small communities that didn't require a passenger train stop and didn't have multiple mail pouches to be loaded and unloaded.

The rack next to the track is called a mail crane, **7**. It was generally located at one end of the station platform. Cranes followed many designs, usually following each railroad's standard design. All held a pouch vertically, so that the top and bottom arms grab the bottom and top of the pouch (it holds it upside down), so the crane will release the pouch as the catcher grabs it.

Trains didn't slow down for this operation, and making the catch at speeds of 60 mph and faster was not unusual. As the train approached the crane, a clerk opened the RPO door and set the catcher in position with the handle. As soon as the hook grabbed the pouch, the clerk removed the pouch from the catcher, retracted the catcher, and brought the pouch into the car to begin working it, **8**.

As this was happening, the clerk also had to throw or kick off the mail sack destined for the station, **9**. He had to make sure the sack was flung far enough from the track that it wasn't drawn back under the train. He also took care not hit anyone on the ground or throw it so far that it took out a window on the station.

There were many dangers and opportunities for the process to go wrong. The clerk had to know just

As the clerk prepares to make the catch, he also kicks or tosses the delivery pouch out the door. This is on the Boston & Maine in the late 1940s. *Edward J. Howard Jr.*

The mail messenger at Bethel, Minn., Phil Fox, hangs the pouch for the approaching Great Northern train in fall 1968. *Don Hofsommer*

Burlington Route heavyweight RPO no. 1914 is 70 feet long with a 30-foot mail apartment. *Hol Wagner*

RPO interiors were built to Post Office specifications. This new ACF car, built in 1950 for Great Northern, displays the cases and pouch racks. *American Car & Foundry*

where he was, as the arm—which extended more than two feet outward from the car—would catch other objects if deployed too soon (poles, bridge abutments, signal masts, cars on parallel tracks, etc.). Whistle or horn signals were given, but these could be difficult to hear. Visibility was especially difficult at night or in fog, snow, rain, or other bad weather.

Clerks had to work quickly, especially when stations were only a few miles apart. This required making a catch, opening that pouch and dumping the contents on a sorting table to see if anything in it was destined for the next town, closing ("locking out") the pouch for the next town in time to make the next drop and catch—and then repeating the process.

The bags used for this were called "catcher pouches." Stronger than standard mail pouches, they were reinforced and had steel rings at each end for attaching to the crane. Mail was placed at both ends of the pouch, with a strap around a middle, to balance the weight.

Pouches were hung by the local postmaster (small towns were often one-person operations) or by a mail messenger (a depot agent might serve this role), **10**. Pouches were supposed to be hung no more than 10 minutes before the scheduled arrival of the train.

RPO and storage cars

Early RPO cars were made of wood, as were other passenger cars. This made them a dangerous place to be in case of wrecks, which were unfortunately all too common in the 1800s. The first danger was the wreck itself, as wood bodies would often disintegrate; the next danger was fire, especially with the use of coal stoves aboard cars.

The first steel mail cars appeared around 1900, originally having steel frames with wood bodies and then as all-steel cars. Wood RPOs were prohibited from service as of 1917.

RPO cars were owned by individual railroads but built to Post Office specifications, **11**. Each RPO car was built in one of three patterns. Full RPO cars had a working area 60 feet long. Smaller RPOs were often combined with baggage or chair cars (called *combines*—these cars had RPO apartments, either 15 or 30 feet long).

As mentioned earlier, cars were equipped with sets of slots or pigeonholes in a prescribed grouping called a case, along with hooks and racks for hanging pouches, **12**. Cars had a lavatory, clothes rack, and drinking water. There was a mail drop (letter slot) on each side.

Although the interior had to follow Post Office specifications, each car was built to each railroad's designs, generally following roof and side patterns to match other passenger cars. Into the 1930s, these were heavyweight cars, usually riding on six-wheel trucks. As streamliners were built with lightweight design, new RPOs followed, with smooth sides or stainless fluting to match the new trains.

As of the mid-1940s, there were about 3,500 RPO cars in service, including 628 full 60-foot cars. The remainder were combines with 30- or 15-foot apartments. The chart on page 83 shows the AAR car classifications for the various types of combination cars.

Storage mail was carried in standard baggage cars, **13**, or express boxcars (see chapter 4), **14**. Some were marked with MAIL STORAGE stenciling or lettering, but any car could be used. Express refrigerator cars were often used for mail storage when not needed for refrigerated shipments, and this was especially common during the Christmas rush.

Mail storage cars had color-coded placards (placed in a holder next to a side door) marked U.S. MAIL with information on the load. Blue placards marked a destination car—these would stay sealed and wouldn't be worked until their destination. White cards indicated a working car—these were the cars that were opened at local stops for mail to be loaded and unloaded. Pink or salmon placards denoted a relay car—these were opened at designated spots to transfer mail (including to or from an RPO).

From the late 1950s onward, truck trailers were often used to carry storage mail, often in piggyback (trailer-on-flatcar) form, **15**. Flexi-Vans—containers on flatcars with separate bogies (wheels) added at terminals to turn them into trailers—were also extensively used for storage mail, **16**. The New York Central was the biggest user, and Milwaukee Road, Santa Fe, Illinois Central, and Burlington were others.

Also worthy of mention are Chesapeake & Ohio's Railvans (later called RoadRailers). These were 26-foot highway trailers equipped with a retractable set of steel flanged wheels at the rear that allowed them to operate on railroad tracks. Introduced in 1956, they were used initially for storage mail service from Detroit to Grand Rapids, Mich., coupled on the ends of passenger trains. They expanded into other routes in Michigan and Indiana, operating into the mid-1960s, **17**.

Train operations

The Post Office could select any railroad to carry storage mail over any route, and awarded contracts to railroads based on speed of operation and on-time delivery. Railroads faced financial penalties for late trains and poor handling, and risked contracts shifting to another railroad if performance wasn't up to par.

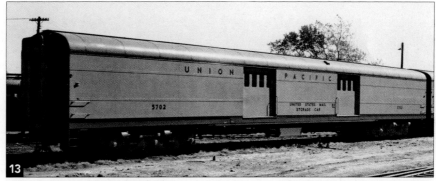

Union Pacific no. 5702 was assigned and lettered as a mail storage car. Built by ACF in 1949, it was a long (85-foot) streamlined lightweight car riding on six-wheel trucks. *Union Pacific*

This Texas & Pacific express boxcar (note the steam and signal lines) is labeled for mail storage and painted in the road's passenger colors. *Roy C. Meates*

The Great Northern used these 36-foot single-axle trailers (with International tractors) to carry mail in Montana from Great Falls to Butte and Billings. *Great Northern*

The Illinois Central was one of several roads that used Flexi-Vans for mail. Here, two Flexi-Van cars (four containers) are tucked behind the engines on the *Land O' Corn* at Rockford, Ill., in March 1967. *Mike Schafer*

Chesapeake & Ohio's 1950s RoadRailers were single-axle highway trailers with built-in rail wheels at the rear, allowing them to operate at the rear of passenger trains. *Chesapeake & Ohio (top), Louis A. Marre collection (bottom)*

Mail contracts were lucrative—they kept passenger operations viable on many routes—so trains carrying large amounts of mail were given preferential operational treatment at or above the level of signature passenger trains.

Along with the RPO cars described earlier, this meant thousands of cars of storage mail traveling around the country. For example, in the 1950s, New York City, the largest mail hub in the country, saw 140 trains a day with RPO cars, plus another 200 mail storage cars. Each storage car ran on a strict schedule, depending upon many connections to get from origination to destination.

To handle this—along with Railway Express Agency traffic—railroads used both their regularly scheduled passenger trains as well as dedicated all-mail/express trains. These sometimes included a single rider coach at the rear, but many had no passenger cars. They weren't listed in public timetables, and the only people aboard were mail clerks and train crew, but they were first-class trains. Many carried the official or unofficial name of *Fast Mail*.

To get an idea of how train operations worked, including connections among trains, let's follow the journeys of several cars across the country from the East Coast to the Midwest and West Coast along several railroads, **18**.

Let's start with New York Central train 13, an all mail and express train (no riders) from Buffalo to Chicago, made up primarily of storage cars originating in New York City and Boston and destined for points west (it was actually only numbered 13 for its last leg into Chicago). It was due into Englewood Station (south of downtown Chicago) at 5:55 p.m.

This train would typically have 20 or more cars of mail and express. The ones we're concerned with are six cars destined for Chicago, Burlington & Quincy No. 29 (the Chicago–Omaha *Fast Mail*, due out of Union Station at 9 p.m.), and eight cars bound for Milwaukee Road No. 57 (the Chicago–Minneapolis *Fast Mail*, also due out of Union Station at 9 p.m.).

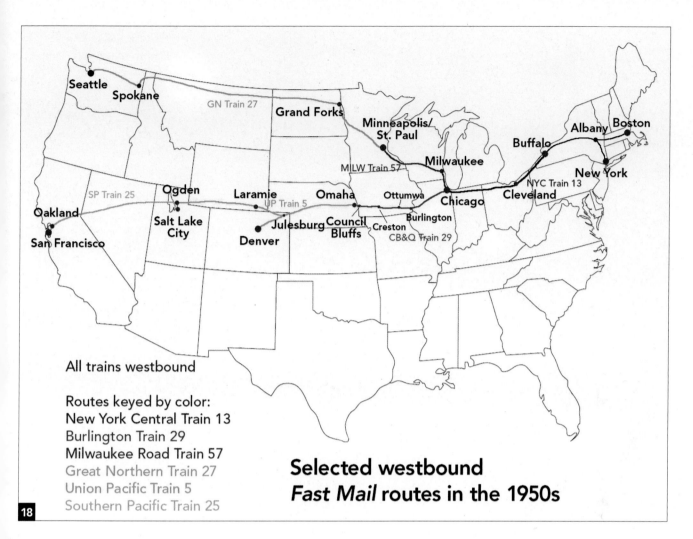

All trains westbound

Routes keyed by color:
New York Central Train 13
Burlington Train 29
Milwaukee Road Train 57
Great Northern Train 27
Union Pacific Train 5
Southern Pacific Train 25

**Selected westbound
Fast Mail routes in the 1950s**

Cars would be placed on the station tracks well before the departure time for both the Milwaukee and Burlington trains, with the working RPOs in place and loaded (and clerks working), along with other storage cars—including those originating at Chicago and coming from other connecting trains, **19**. Some time after 7 p.m., a switcher would arrive with the connecting cars from NYC No. 13 (Englewood was several miles south of Union Station), **20**.

For Burlington train 29, this included express and mail cars bound for Oakland, express and mail cars for Denver, and mail cars for Council Bluffs and Omaha (all headed for the Union Pacific). From train 13, the Milwaukee Road gets mail and express cars bound for St. Paul, Spokane, and Seattle, plus an express car for Milwaukee.

Let's follow CB&Q No. 29. It pulls out of Union Station on time at 9 p.m.,

with two E units pulling 15 head-end cars and no passenger cars. It has eight hours to travel 470 miles to Omaha for its scheduled 5 a.m. arrival. En route, No. 29 will set out cars at Burlington, Ottumwa, Creston, and multiple cars at Council Bluffs for the Union Pacific Transfer, a huge mail-handling terminal in Council Bluffs. It will also pause to load and unload multiple bags of mail at several other stations.

On board, the RPO clerks work mail for dozens of Iowa cities as well as Omaha and other points to the west. Number 29 did not make these drop-offs, however. Instead, Iowa pouches would be left at Council Bluffs, where the eastbound *Denver Zephyr* would do that job in the morning.

By the time No. 29 ties up at Omaha, its clerks will have worked more than 400 pouches of mail. At Omaha, several cars (including four from NYC No. 13 and additional cars from Chicago) will be switched to UP

train No. 5 (the *Mail and Express*) to continue westward. Cars set out at the Transfer will have their sacks sorted and loaded for their next journeys on any of seven railroads that use the facility.

The UP will hand off its Oakland-bound cars from New York to Southern Pacific train 25 at Ogden for the last leg of their journey to the coast.

While No. 29 was doing its thing, Milwaukee No. 57 was carrying its cars from Chicago to Minneapolis, setting out and picking up cars at four locations and pausing at five others to drop off and pick up mail bags, with its clerks working mail all the way. Number 57 pulled into Minneapolis at 6:15, handing off several westbound cars to Great Northern train 27 (called, of course, the *Fast Mail*) in time for its 9:30 a.m. departure, **21**. These included the Spokane- and Seattle-bound cars from NYC 13, which No. 27 will deliver on day 2 of its 1,400-plus mile journey.

Workers load mail onto the RPO and storage cars of Burlington No. 29, the *Fast Mail*, prior to its 9 p.m. departure from Chicago Union Station in the early 1960s. *John Gruber*

A switcher tacks a head-end car to a train consist in the wee hours at Portland, Ore., in 1948. *Robert Gazay*

Mail and express storage cars could be lettered for several railroads, as cars were handled over multiple lines. On Burlington's No. 29, for example, you might see cars from the Burlington (including RPO), Pennsylvania or New York Central (mail cars from New York), Union Pacific, and Southern Pacific.

Additional operations

Many other trains carried mail and express traffic. Even front-line name trains carried an RPO; others hauled multiple baggage express and express refrigerator cars. For example, on the same route as Burlington No. 29, CB&Q No. 11 (the Chicago-Lincoln *Nebraska Zephyr*), one day in 1962, had nine head-end cars in addition to its seven-car articulated consist: an RPO, four sealed cars for Omaha (including an Atlantic Coast Line car), a sealed SP car for Oakland, and two sealed cars for Lincoln.

Trains, of course, don't always run on time. At large terminals, transfer clerks were in charge of making sure mail (or entire mail cars) got from one railroad to another to make connections. This could be a challenge depending upon how far apart the depots and terminals were, how tight the connection were, and how late a train was.

Depending upon the situation, an outbound train might be held; otherwise, the mail or cars would have to be placed on another train. If several cars were involved, the departing train may be sent in separate sections.

The weeks leading to Christmas were the busiest time for mail and express traffic, with a huge influx of letters and parcels. Railroads would be forced to press all available equipment into service, **22**. Trains (standard passenger trains as well as mail and express trains) were often run in multiple sections, with additional RPO cars added.

As with freight trains, cars in mail/express trains would be blocked if possible. This means that cars for common destinations would be grouped together to make switching faster at the next location. In the earlier example of NYC train 13, the cars destined for the Burlington would be grouped together; likewise the cars bound for the Milwaukee would also be grouped together.

Terminal switch crews would place and pull cars as needed from station tracks, often moving them from an arrival track to the nearby post office or express building (or vice versa), **23**. They might also have to pull cars to another nearby station or yard if a car was being interchanged with another railroad.

Terminal switchers also had to be aware of special needs. For example, Santa Fe's Chicago to Los Angeles Train No. 7 (the *Fast Mail Express*) had two RPO cars. They had to have their working ends together so each had access to storage cars on the other end. On occasion, an RPO would have to be turned on a turntable to get it ready because an unknowing switch crew put them together incorrectly.

Great Northern train 27, that railroad's *Fast Mail*, departs the Twin Cities with its load of head-end traffic bound for Seattle in the early 1960s. Trains *magazine collection*

A long string of Pacific Fruit Express reefers are being loaded with mail at right as workers sort mail bags at the Union Pacific Transfer in Council Bluffs, Iowa, during the 1951 Christmas rush. *Union Pacific Museum*

A New Orleans Union Passenger Terminal switcher shoves a string of head-end cars toward the terminal in April 1954. *James G. LaVake*

Bibliography

Books

The American Railroad Passenger Car, by John H. White Jr., Johns Hopkins University Press, 1985

Express Business in the U. S. in 1907, by Russell H. Snead, U. S. Bureau of the Census, 1907

From Rail to Road and Back Again, edited by Ralf Roth and Colin Divall, Dorset Press, 2015

Model Railroader's Guide to Passenger Equipment & Operations, by Andy Sperandeo, Kalmbach Publishing Co., 2006

Moving Mail and Express by Rail, by Edward M. DeRouin, Pixels Publishing, 2007

New York Central Railroad, by Brian Solomon with Mike Schaefer, Voyageur Press (MBI), 2007

Railway Express: An Overview, by V. S. Roseman, Rocky Mountain Publishing, 1992

St. Paul Union Depot, by John W. Diers, University of Minnesota Press, 2013

Southern Pacific's Blue Streak Merchandise, by Fred W. Frailey, Kalmbach Publishing Co., 1991

Ten Turtles to Tucumcari, by Klink Garrett with Toby Smith, University of New Mexico Press, 2003

Periodicals

"The Big Mail Drop," by Harry L. Tennant, *Modern Railroads,* September 1967

"Boston-Seattle for 3¢" [mail by rail], by David A. Thompson, *Classic Trains,* Fall 2006

"BR and BS Express Refrigerator Cars," by Pat Wider, *Railway Prototype Cyclopedia,* Vol. 7 (2002)

"Crescent City Nirvana" (New Orleans Union Passenger Terminal), by C. K. Marsh Jr., *Classic Trains,* Winter 2006

"Decline and Decay of REA," by Robert B. Shaw, *Trains,* July 1979

"Eagle Merchandise Service," by Charles Duckworth, *Missouri Pacific Historical Society Eagle,* Spring 1997

"The Fast Mail" [Milwaukee Road], by William F. Stauss, *The Milwaukee Railroader* (Milwaukee Road Historical Association), June 1989

"The Fast Mail Express," by John R. Signor and Dave Lambert, *Warbonnet* (Santa Fe Railway Historical and Modeling Society), Second Quarter 1997

"Fast Mail, The First 75 Years," by David P. Morgan, *Classic Trains,* Fall 2006

"The Fast Ones: BX Express Boxcars," by Pat Wider, *Railway Prototype Cyclopedia,* Vol. 6 [plus addendum in Vol. 8]

"The Few, The Proud" [RPO service], by Peter A. Hansen, *Classic Trains,* Fall 2006

"Freight Houses and LCL Don't Get No Respect," by Mark Vaughan, *The Banner* (Wabash Railroad Historical Society), No. 70 (July 2010)

"Great Northern Head-End Cars Part VI: Express Refrigerator Cars," by John R. Westley, Great Northern Ry. Historical Society Reference Sheet No. 165 (1990)

"Great Northern Railway Mail Services," by Stuart Holmquist, Great Northern Ry. Historical Society Reference Sheet No. 177 (1991)

"Great Northern's Rider-Storage Mail Cars," by Kurt E. Armbruster, Great Northern Ry. Historical Society Reference Sheet No. 291 (2001)

"Handling Express by Tractor and Trailer," *Railway Age,* Nov. 26, 1927

"Handling Freight in the Country's Largest Terminal" (PRR Polk Street), *Railway Age,* Jan. 21, 1922

"Head-End Equipment and Operations," by Paul J. Dolkos, *Model Railroader,* August and September 2007 [two parts]

"Holiday Mail Operation 1959," by Dave Seidel, *Union Pacific Historical Society Streamliner,* Vol. 21, No. 4, Fall 2007

"Loading Guides Solve Difficulties of L.C.L. Freight," *Railway Age,* Dec. 24, 1921

"The Mail is Coming," by David A. Thompson, *Minnesota History* (Minnesota Historical Society), Spring 2015

"Mail on the Rails," by V. S. Roseman, *Model Railroader,* July 2004

"Modern Methods of Handling Package Freight, by G. Marks, *Railway Age,* Feb. 25, 1922

"Operating a Modern Freight House Efficiently," by W. E. Phelps, *Railway Age,* Jan. 14, 1921

"Pacemaker Fast Freight Service," by Lawrence R. Bolton, *Central Headlight* (New York Central System Historical Society), First Quarter 1992

"Is the Post Office Fooling Itself?" *Railway Age,* Oct. 18, 1954

"Profit Motive to the Rescue" (REA), *Business Week,* Dec. 8, 1962

"Racing Into History" (RPO service), by Don L. Hofsommer, *Classic Trains,* Fall 2006

"Rail-Highway Coordination No Longer Experimental," *Railway Age*, Jan. 26, 1935

"Railway Express Expands Use of Piggyback," *Modern Railroads*, April 1960

"Railway Mail Service on the Burlington," by Hol Wagner, *Burlington Route Historical Society Bulletin*, No. 8 (1983)

"The Railway Post Office on the Union Pacific Railroad," by Kenton H. Forrest, *Union Pacific Historical Society Streamliner*, Vol. 12, No. 2, Spring 1998

"Rutland LCL," by Bob Nimke, *Rutland Railroad Historical Society Newsliner*, Winter 1991

"Santa Fe's Newest Rail-Truck Terminal Opens at Kansas City," *Railway Age*, April 3, 1961

"Story of the Railway Mail Service," by R. W. Marks, *Chicago & Eastern Illinois Railroad Employees' Magazine*, August 1946

"Survival Fight Won, REA Aims to Prosper," *Railway Age*, Jan. 28, 1963.

"UP Express Boxcars," by D. W. Dickerhoof, *Union Pacific Historical Society Streamliner*, Vol. 5, No. 4 (1989)

"When LCL Meant Fast Freight," by Charles W. Bohi, *Trains*, August 1993

Pamphlets, brochures, and miscellany

"Express Troopers Revisited," by Dave Lambert, Railroad Prototype Modelers seminar, Naperville, 2005

The Most Mail for the Least Money, *Association of American Railroads*

Nelson's Encyclopedia, Vol. 4, 1929

Railroad Car Facts, American Railway Car Institute, 1961

"The Railway Express Story," Proceedings: The Journal of the Pacific Railway Club, Vol. 24, No. 8, November 1940

The Railway Mail Story, American Association of Railroads, 1957

Car Builders' Cyclopedia, various editions

The Freight Traffic Red Book, various editions

The Official Guide of the Railways, various editions

The Official Railway Equipment Register, various editions

Railway Engineering & Maintenance Cyclopedia, various editions

Thanks and acknowledgments

Thanks to the following people who provided photos, information, and other material for the book: Ted Culotta, Cody Grivno, J. David Ingles, Russ MacNeil, Robert S. McGonigal, Robert Milner, Tom Hoffman, Kevin Keefe, Gary Rich, Toby Smith, Hank Suderman, and David Thompson.

Many spent significant time digging up photos and compiling information for me, and this book would not have been completed without their efforts.

I'm grateful I was able to use several photos taken by my friend, the late Ed DeRouin, and use the outstanding reference he compiled: *Moving Mail and Express by Rail*. I also thank all of the photographers whose works reside in the David P. Morgan Library at Kalmbach Publishing Co. Without that amazing library as a resource, this book would not have been possible.

In compiling this book I used hundreds of sources, including books, magazines, trade publications, historical society publications, railroad press releases and publications, photographs, timetables, brochures, and various websites. There were many places where information conflicted, such as dates and rosters. I made my best effort to determine what was correct, and any mistakes that remain are my own.

— *Jeff Wilson*

Great Books to Help
ADD REALISM
TO YOUR LAYOUTS!

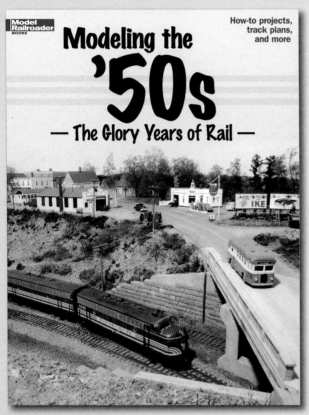

Model Railroader BOOKS

How-to projects, track plans, and more

Modeling the '50s
— The Glory Years of Rail —

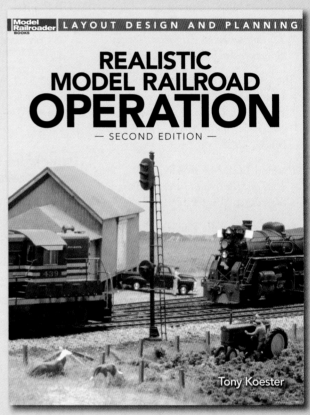

Model Railroader BOOKS LAYOUT DESIGN AND PLANNING

REALISTIC MODEL RAILROAD OPERATION
— SECOND EDITION —

Tony Koester

Readers interested in modeling a realistic railroad of the 1950s will love this book based on a special 2005 issue of *Model Railroader*. This book provides historical information and photos covering locomotives, passenger equipment, freight cars, and trackside details. Featured layouts in a variety of scales show how to model Chicago's Dearborn Station, move coal in the Appalachians, carry produce, and recreate Los Angeles of the 1950s.

12456 • $19.95

Respected expert Tony Koester teaches modelers how real railroads operate trains and how to apply those methods to their own model railroads in this extensively updated edition. Learning about timetable-and-train-order operation, as well as how cars are switched, how yards function, how signals work, and more, provides an added dimension of realism and fun for modelers, keeping the hobby fresh and exciting.

12480 • $19.95

Buy now from your local hobby shop!
Shop at KalmbachHobbyStore.com

P28557